MY FAILINGS AND IMPERFECTIONS
The Diary of Rees Thomas of Dôl-llan, 1860–1862

January 1860

1860

Vol 1st By reflecting upon my
C + the last year, & the reckoning
of the number of hours spared for
mental cultivation, together with
the amount spent ~~upon~~ in consequence of my occasional fits of inte-
perance, also I find that all my failings
+ imperfections is are entirely attributed to alcoholic drink, & to that
alone, therefore why is it that I ever
taste a single drop, of such poison
when I plainly see & find & that it
not merely deprive me of a large
amount of money every year, but
I as been heretofore the ruin of
morals as well as my character in
the eyes of others, for I am spoken
of in the neighbourhood, as a com
plete Drunkard & that had it not
been for that, I should have been
an useful member to society

Diary first page.
(Photograph: Steve Dubé, courtesy of Pembrokeshire Record Office).

MY FAILINGS AND IMPERFECTIONS

The Diary of Rees Thomas of Dôl-llan, 1860–1862

Editor:

STEVE DUBÉ

Best wishes

Steve Dubé

Published by

Cymdeithas Hanes Ceredigion/Ceredigion Historical Society

and

Cymdeithas Hynafiaethau Sir Gaerfyrddin/Carmarthenshire Antiquarian Society

Published by
Cymdeithas Hanes Ceredigion/Ceredigion Historical Society
and
Cymdeithas Hynafiaethau Sir Gaerfyrddin/Carmarthenshire Antiquarian Society

ISBN 978-0-906972-07-6

Printed in Wales by
Dinefwr Press
Rawlings Road, Llandybie
Carmarthenshire, SA18 3YD

Contents

Acknowledgements

It was a reference in Leslie Baker-Jones' exploration of the Tivyside gentry in his book *Princelings, Privilege and Power* that first took me to the pages of the Rees Thomas diary, and he subsequently gave freely of his time and his knowledge of his native valley to help me to compile this book. Thomas Lloyd offered leads, illustrations and frequent encouragement. Alan Griffiths at Dôl-llan and Gwenllian Kidd at Llanfair were welcoming and gave invaluable assistance. The staff at the National Library of Wales, and the Record Offices in Haverfordwest and Carmarthen, were a great help. Dr John Cule and Dr Harold Selcon both helped me to get to grips with medical matters. Michael Freeman offered valuable advice at an important stage in the proceedings. I thank them all. Thanks also to Eddie John at Dinefwr Press for advice, professionalism and attention to detail. But above all my partner Janet delivered practical help with research, along with advice, encouragement, forbearance and love.

The diary of Rees Thomas and associated documents and ephemera were deposited in Pembrokeshire Record Office by R. T. P. Williams, Solicitors, of Haverfordwest, who granted permission to publish.

ILLUSTRATIONS

Courtesy of, or photographs by: Steve Dubé
                                  Thomas Lloyd
                                  Gwenllian Kidd.

Photographs of the diary itself: Pembrokeshire Record Office.

FRONT COVER

Llandyssil 1813 by John George Wood in *Principal Rivers of Wales*,
published in 1813.

Foreword

This remarkable diary, which has only survived by luck, gives a vivid insight into a lifestyle far from unique but seldom recorded. And especially not in such searing honesty and detail.

Rees Thomas was born into that seemingly fortunate station of being a gentleman, but yet a younger son of a family of such relatively modest fortune that he was trapped in a way of life that could not sustain him. He had clearly been properly educated and so could have trained and worked in one of the professions, such as the law or medicine, which were respectable for a more motivated gentleman of limited private means. But like many, Rees preferred to try and live at leisure on the tiny estate his father had bequeathed him, a victim of the snobberies of Victorian stratified society. We only have this one brief diary, out of what might have been a more revealing sequence, but by 1860, his die was cast, and unhappiness and batchelorhood had forced him into the clutches of the demon drink – and into the arms of his not always willing servants.

The lifestyle of the grandest in society is well recorded. But the further down the scale, where most people lived, the less we have. From watching period dramas on the television, we naturally imagine a gentleman to be finely turned out and mannered, yet in the deeper country, such as in this instance around Llandysul, there would be respectable tenant farmers whose lifestyle was more comfortable than the poorer gentry. Rees talks to his diary as a way of finding solace and to set in words his promises for self-improvement, which alas, never seem to happen.

Apart from the excerpt from the one act tragedy that these pages present, the reader is allowed many valuable sidelights on the local events of the day. When fit enough to be out and about, Rees was an active member of society in the area around Llandysul and comments keenly on events, giving us vital information on a long lost way of life and flourishing local community.

It is therefore greatly to our benefit that Steve Dubé has spent many hours transcribing Rees's difficult hand and the coded allusions to his behaviour. He has researched and footnoted extensively all the passing references to people and events, greatly enhancing the diary entries. The Carmarthenshire Antiquarian Society and Ceredigion Historical Society (which have come together for this joint publication) thank him most sincerely for this valuable addition to knowledge on their mutual borders.

THOMAS LLOYD, FSA
Wales Herald Extraordinary
Vice President, Carmarthenshire Antiquarian Society

Introduction

On New Year's Day 1860 the 36-year-old yeoman farmer and landowner Rees Thomas sat at his desk in his "most delightful residence"[1] and opened a small soft-cover maroon notebook. He inked his quill pen and wrote the month and year in English at the top of the page. Then he wrote the day, Sunday, in Latin – Sol 1st – and began as follows: *"By reflecting upon my Conduct in the last year & the reckoning of the number of hours spared for mental cultivation, together with the amount spent in consequence of my occasional fits of intemperance also, I find that all my failings and imperfections are entirely attributed to alcoholic drink and to that alone, therefore why is it that I ever taste a single drop of such poison when I plainly see and find that it not merely deprive me of a large amount of money every year but has been heretofore the ruin of morals as well as my character in the eyes of others as I am spoken of in the neighbourhood as a complete Drunkard and that had it not been for that I should have been an useful member of society, therefore I shall henceforth be a teetotaller."*[2] And, perhaps returning to the top of the page – the writing is smaller – and perhaps in hope as much as expectation, he adds the word "teetotaler" [sic] and underlines it.

It is an explosive opening that shows us straight away that this is no mere chronicle of someone's life. This is a sort of confessional, the type of diary that amounts to emotional striptease and that can make uncomfortable voyeurs of us. And it's not often that we find such frankness and exposure in a voice that comes from what might be described as a non-artistic section of society. This diary is no aide memoire or catalogue of engagements and events. There are fascinating insights into how people lived in Victorian Wales, but the overwhelming impression is of unbuttoned stuff. The period of two years and eight months recorded here is written in the voice of a painfully honest man, whose plaintive mix of shame and resolve is repeated many times in a diary that he kept, day by day without a break, until the end of August, 1862. For, among other things, Rees was a binge alcoholic, unable to stop once he had started, and repeatedly drinking himself into a stupor that lasted several days and left him debilitated and consumed with regret.

The squire of Dôl-llan in the north Carmarthenshire parish of Llanfihangel ar Arth was not unusual among his contemporaries. *"The Welsh squirearchy has been often reproached with drunkenness . . ."*[3] wrote Herbert Millingchamp Vaughan (1870–1948), who defined a squire as someone owning a mansion or residence with a home farm attached and an estate with tenants.[4]

Vaughan himself was squire of Llangoedmor near Cardigan, and his *South Wales Squires*, published in 1926, is an important insider's account written at a time when the position and power of the landed gentry had already been diminished by the County Council Act of 1887. The complete demise of the Welsh squirearchy was to follow after World War One when heavy taxes, rising costs and falling income led to widespread abandonment and sale of estates.

---

1. Dolellan Sale catalogue, 16 August 1887, Carmarthen Record Office.
2. Diary, 1 January 1860.
3. Hebert M. Vaughan, *The South Wales Squires*, Methuen, 1926, p. 108.
4. Ibid., pp. 1 to 4.

1

Vaughan insisted the drink problem was no greater among the gentry than in any other stratum of society, but blamed the custom among the gentry of giving children wine with their dessert for the creation of so many "human slaves to drink".[5] He illustrated the widespread nature of alcohol misuse by recalling the way his mother used to respond to his own "irritating childish persistence" in asking what sort of man a neighbour was. The answer "invariably" was "very nice *except for one little failing*".[6] Rees Thomas was evidently such a man.

His home at Dôl-llan, which translates as "church meadow", was a small mansion, possibly remodelled by – or at least in the style of – the Regency architect John Nash,[7] which took its name from its location just across the River Teifi and a wide meadow's width from the parish church of Llandysul. His estate was relatively modest. Just 35 acres were attached to Dôl-llan itself.[8] But at least 300 acres went with the farms of Dolygrogws, Dôl-llan Ucha (now known as Farmyard), and Ffynnonbwla,[9] which Rees also inherited from his father.[10] He was a yeoman squire who, as the diary shows, would join his workers in the fields.

His social status was at the lower end of the west Wales gentry – without being considered, by the gentry at least, among their ranks – but his background was highly respected. He was a younger son of Llanfair, a mansion and estate less than a mile away, and his family had an illustrious pedigree. Rees with his five brothers and one sister were direct descendents of Jenkin Jones (1700?–1742), founder of the Unitarian Chapel at Llwynrhydowen and one of the biggest names in the history of Unitarianism in the Teifi Valley. And through their great-great-grandfather, the Rev'd David Lloyd of Llwynrhydowen and Brynllefrith (1724–1779), who married his first cousin Jane (daughter of Jenkin Jones) they traced their lineage back through the Castell Hywel and Alltrodyn families to the great Welsh warrior Cadifor ap Dinawel.[11] This was the man who in 1164 commanded Welsh soldiers in a siege of Cardigan Castle, which he took from a force of Normans and Flemings under Roger, Earl of Clare, by leading his men up ladders and over the walls. In reward Cadifor was granted the lordships and lands of Castle Hywel, Pantstrimon and Gilfachwen by his kinsman, the Lord Rhys ap Gruffydd, Prince of South Wales, and given the hand of Rhys's daughter Catherine in marriage. Descendents still held those lands, and the Thomas coat of arms, assigned to Rees' nephews David and John Thomas in 1874, included two "scaling ladders sable" in commemoration of the event.[12] The family's best known descendent was the great American architect Frank Lloyd Wright (1867–1959). He and Rees Thomas were third cousins.

In the Unitarian sphere the Thomas family had endowed several chapels and provided some notable ministers. The closest link was with Pantydefaid Chapel, the family's place of worship at Prengwyn, built on a plot of land given by their ancestor, Jenkin Jones.[13] The family was later instrumental in securing an adjoining plot of land as a burial ground and the chapel has two windows

---

5. Ibid., p. 109.
6. Ibid.
7. See Appendix 1.
8. 1861 Census, Llanfihangel ar Arth.
9. Ibid.
10. Will of David Thomas of Llanfair (1784–1845). NLW Morgan Richardson Papers, Llanfair Deeds & Documents, 1761–1908, 1111–1112.
11. Lineage of the Family of Thomas of Ffos Esgob and Llanfair, both in the Parish of Llandyssul in the County of Carmarthen, Pembrokeshire Record Office, HRO D/Wil/197; George Eyre Evans (editor), *Lloyd Letters, 1908.*
12. W. J. Davies, *Hanes Plwyf Llandyssul*, Gwasg Gomer, p. 228.
13. D. Elwyn Davies, *They Thought for Themselves*, 1982, printed by Gomer Press, p. 43.

commemorating family members.[14] The close connection with the Unitarian cause was sustained by Rees Thomas's uncle, the Rev'd Thomas Thomas, Llanfair, who was regarded as an outstanding minister and teacher. When he died before his 29th birthday in August, 1818, he was buried beneath the communion table at Pantydefaid Chapel.[15] In the diary, ministers and clergy are frequent visitors at Llanfair and Dôl-llan, often staying for several days. One example is July 1860 when nearly three weeks were taken up with guests including a Minister from Tavistock, a Church of England curate, the Principal of the Presbyterian College at Carmarthen and his family and the daughters of the Rector of a neighbouring parish.

So Rees had a lot to live up to and a status to maintain, and the standard of English in the diary – and his use of Latin to delineate the days of the week – suggests he had been educated to a level considered appropriate to his social standing. It was an expectation that weighed heavily, especially because, as his diary shows, the Thomas family, for all its status and material advantage, was as dysfunctional as any in the mid 19th century.

That first entry in the diary sets a tone that would underlie the record of those two years and eight months. The entry ends, as did most of the entries he was to write, with a private code and the word "unavoidably." As it is impossible to decipher the code – it may relate to pharmaceutical drugs or potions – these code words have been edited out of this transcript. And missing letters have been inserted into half-written words for readability's sake. Like many other diarists, Rees makes frequent use of code or gobbledygook to describe things he wished to hide from anyone who might come by chance upon his little book, and he left blank spaces in words he could not bring himself to write out in full. But he was frank about his drinking and the shame he felt to his self-esteem and social standing. Like a good diarist he wrote it all down but unlike many diaries from Victorian times this is no repetitive list of activities and has not suffered from censorship imposed by a relative or descendant for decency's sake. This diary is sometimes raw and always frank, a revealing expression of the inner man.

He recorded his alcoholic binges with a thinly disguised "Int" or "Into", for intoxicated. For instance on New Year's Day, 1861, Thomas wrote – "Funeral of Twmi Daniel..Into." This was Thomas Rees, a tailor and "a worthy friend", who had been ill for some years. The occasion led to three days where the diary contains only the single shortened word for drunk. On the fourth day of his binge he needs a visit from the doctor. The fifth day reads (with allowances for his crude shorthand), "Half dead, getting Sober" and the sixth has the single-word entry "Bewildered" – a description that invariably follows his binges.

In this Rees is like another squire from earlier times who also recorded his weakness for alcohol in a diary. George Hilton (1673–1725), of the now ruinous Beetham Hall in the Cumbrian village of Beetham just north of the Lancashire border, represented his "fuddle" days, as he called them, by a series of asterisks in his diary.[16] Hilton was also ashamed of his habit, admitting *"I have often lost my reason by immoderate drinking."* He adds: *"I am most passionately resolved to have soe punctuall a gaurd over my inclynacion as never to loose my reason by immoderate drinking."* [Original spelling throughout.] Hilton does "loose" his reason and often becomes violent, a tendency not helped by his habit of carrying a sword, a whip and a riding crop. He was always getting into fights and ending up in court, and on one occasion left a man blinded in one eye.

14. Ibid., p. 45.
15. W. J. Davies, p. 205.
16. *The Rake's Diary, the Journal of George Hilton*, Curwen Archives Trust, 1994.

Rees, as far as we know, was never moved to violence through drink, although he contemplated it in exasperation once or twice as he wrote up his diary. And a century and a half after Hilton, Rees Thomas also resolves to forsake the demon. At regular intervals and on occasions solemnly on the Bible and in front of his best friend (and tenant) Evan Griffiths of Dolgrogws, he pledges never to drink again. On 25 November, 1860, he writes: *"This day for the last time I swore on the New Testament . . . that I should abstain entirely from tasting a drop of any intoxicating beverages from today to the 31st of December 1861. The oath is written on a paper to be read every morning . . . May the Almighty God assist me to observe it."* On 22 December 1960 after a busy day meeting solicitors and bankers in Carmarthen, he records that he is *"most happy owing that I had not tasted a drop of any intoxicating beverages all day."* But on Boxing Day, 26 December, he drank *"Ginger resin wine at the Druggist & Tyssil Castle till quite drunk and consequently made a complete fool of myself."* Rees is locked into the classic behaviour of the binge alcoholic, repeatedly revisiting his nemesis when overcome by stress, emotion or simple temptation. But unlike Hilton, Rees was a danger only to himself.

Much of his stress relates to legal matters. Like many of the squires and gentry of west Wales, the Thomas family was entangled in complicated lawsuits, often concerned with disputed wills and legacies and frequently with each other. At least one of these was only finally settled long after Rees' death.[17] This shows that Rees Thomas, as sole executor of his brother Thomas' will, failed to raise legacies from the Llanfair estate and distribute them to family members. It was not for want of trying. The diary records long days poring over the books of the Llanfair estate and wrestling with its debts and other family matters. Rees was only the third son of his parents David and Mary Thomas, but he found himself head of the family. His eldest brother, Thomas, died on 11 February 1860, soon after Rees began his diary (and Rees gives us a detailed account of his brother's last days – right down to his last breath). The second eldest son, John, a surgeon (doctor) of Tyssul Castle, had died a bachelor in 1858.

There were also the incessant demands of those who were owed money by Rees' mother or brothers and sometimes members of the extended family. It seems likely that Rees trained as an accountant – he was elected a permanent auditor of the accounts of the Llandyssil Literary and Scientific Institution in 1855[18] – another reason perhaps why it fell to him to attempt to untangle the family's affairs and act as executor to his relatives' wills. So Rees Thomas effectively controlled the family's affairs, right down to arranging the education of his late brother's five young orphaned children. They are sent to school in places like Bristol and Chester. He seems to have acted with some firmness – perhaps even intransigence – leaving him distrusted and disliked by most of his relatives. The Rev'd Evan Evans of Llaethliw near Aberaeron, brother-in-law of Rees's dead brother Thomas, and legally appointed guardian of the five children, is always looking for money. The Rev'd Evan Evans does not appear to have exercised his guardianship in any way and it is left to Rees Thomas to deal with the legal niceties of the will of Evans' uncle Jenkin Beynon on behalf of his orphaned nephews and nieces, who are legatees. The case is in Chancery and is not settled until after Rees's death. The children, who live mostly with his youngest brother, Jenkin, at Tyssul Castle (now known as Cae'r Bryn) by Llandysul Bridge, appear to hate him for the control he exercises over their affairs, particularly their education. His younger brother David, who eventually moves

---

17. NLW Morgan Richardson Papers, ibid., 1199.
18. *Carmarthen Journal*, 16 February 1855.

into Dôl-llan, is also a headache – a man with severe psychiatric problems and given to violent tantrums, who later ended up in the lunatic asylum in Carmarthen, where he died in 1876.[19] Even his mother, who lives in the house adjoining Dôl-llan, seems to dislike her son. At one point Rees writes: *"I am almost driven to a hopeless state by all the trouble I have in my capacity as an executor & my brother David's affairs, also my mother's as well."*[20]

Then there are the servants. At one stage his two maidservants go on strike and Rees records on several occasions that he went to bed hungry because no one prepared his dinner. He is determined to sack them, but like his frequent resolutions to give up drinking, he finds it hard to put actions to his words. There are indications that his relationship with the most difficult of them, Betsy, was also sexual. Certainly he regrets her eventual departure and writes to her after she is gone. And he does sleep with her replacement, Anne Thomas, and later with Anne's successor Hannah (and gets her pregnant). In this, as in his drinking, Rees is is like many of his contemporaries. Herbert M. Vaughan writes that *"Old Mr Thomas Lloyd of Coedmore, the Whig Lord Lieutenant of Cardiganshire . . . was notorious in a free-and-easy age and society for the number of his bastards . . ."*[21] Vaughan said Lloyd, who died in 1857 and was also a notorious drinker, was quite open about his promiscuity, employing several of his illegitimate children as servants and providing generously for a succession of mistresses. Historians such as Leslie Baker-Jones[22] and Russell Davies[23] also refer to upstairs-downstairs liaisons, and the efforts sometimes made to avoid unwanted consequences. Unlike the example of "Old Mr Thomas Lloyd of Coedmore", these relationships were not generally in the open. But there is evidence that they were normal – sometimes even expected by both master and servant. One classic example is recorded by the Rev'd David Lloyd of Brynllefrith, Rees Thomas' great-great-grandfather, in a letter to his brother Posthumus Lloyd, dated June 13, 1760.[24] It refers to the squire of Cwrt Farm, Cwrtnewydd, one of the houses, as it happens, referenced frequently in the Rees Thomas diary. David Lloyd writes: *"You may remember to have heard when in ye country that Thomas David John of Court Newydd kept a Miss yt went by ye name of Mary Tŷn-y-ffordd, alias Mary Tŷn-y-parc. He has had by this woman 3 or 4 children (besides supposed miscarriages), whom he used to convey to Nurses at a Distance, and ye old woman his wife never the wiser."* Only one week after his wife's death, John of Court Newydd installs his mistress and their children in the family home. This is by no means an atypical example. There were many others, and "Old Mr Thomas Lloyd" was not alone in openly acknowledging illegitimate offspring – though it sometimes only happened posthumously, and often only when the will was read.

Shunned by his family – *"an outcast"* he writes at one point[25] – Rees seeks comfort with his maid servants – and some of his neighbours. Alas for his peace of mind his behaviour clashes strongly with the expectations forced upon him by his social status, the mores of his times and his religion. He seems to come closest of all to Anne Thomas, who he first notices as a servant at Llanfair. He engages her as a house maid after his brother's death and sleeps with her two months to the day after she arrives at Dôl-llan. He writes after one lovemaking: *"Somehow or other I feel l o – e for*

19. H. R. Evans, 'A Village Worthy', *Ceredigion*, Vol. IV, No. 2, p. 172.
20. Diary, 13 March 1860.
21. Herbert M. Vaughan, *The South Wales Squires*, p. 100.
22. Leslie Baker-Jones, *Princelings, Privilege and Power, The Tivyside Gentry in their Community*, Gomer, 1999, pp. 202-213.
23. Russell Davies, *Secret Sins – Sex, Violence and Society in Carmarthenshire, 1870–1920*, University of Wales Press, 1996, pp. 157–185.
24. George Eyre Evans (editor), *Lloyd Letters (1754–1795)*, Aberystwyth, 1908.
25. Diary, 13 July 1960.

S[ervan]t Anne"[26] – a poignant illustration of the social conditioning that prevents him from writing the words "servant" and "love" conventionally and in full. He cannot quite admit his feelings, even to the faithful and non-judgemental ear of his diary.

The affair is evidently intense but Anne eventually leaves, apparently to go to her brothers in Yorkshire, despite his appeals for her to stay. The diary suggests an intense emotional struggle. Anne seems to be a bit of a stunner. Young men come courting and she has a fiancé. Rees is jealous when she leaves the house and constantly mistrusts her, suspecting at one point that she is trying to have his baby, presumably to secure an annual income. They sleep together almost right up to Anne's departure – and the day she leaves Rees sleeps with one of the new servants, Hannah, who had only arrived at Dôl-llan the previous day. And even while his affair with Hannah continues – leading eventually to her becoming pregnant – Rees confesses that he cannot stop thinking about Anne: *"My thoughts still take a very often flight to the b[o]s[o]m of my old S[ervan]t A. No 3 consecutive hours yet passed without the above taking place,"* he writes on one occasion[27] – immediately before climbing into bed again with Hannah.

Whether for love or simple physical relief, and whether with neighbours – he records having sex with several of them – or with servants, Rees notes each occasion in a thinly disguised code which I have rendered in typeface as "com Idt Ls". And he even records, bluntly and with scant disguise, whether he was successful in practising *coitus interruptus*. It doesn't always work, and he has to pay the local doctor to try to effect an abortion for Hannah, without success. In August, 1862, he hands over £7.5s for one year's maintenance of their child and resolves, yet again, "to lead a better life."

Rees is as frank about his sex life as he is about his drinking, and in this there are parallels with another 19th century Carmarthenshire diarist, Thomas Jenkins of Llandeilo,[28] who also uses a code to indicate his liaisons. Jenkins continued to have sex with his servant despite being deeply infatuated with another woman. He has a child by one servant, Jane Thomas, and agrees to pay maintenance. And he later marries another servant, Ann Thomas, with whom he had been having an affair. Examples of sex between master and servant are also found in the famous diaries of Samuel Pepys (1633–1703), among others. Like Rees, Pepys disguises intimate details, in his case using a cocktail of languages. Sylas Neville (1741–1840) insists to his diary that although some observers might be "censorious" at his decision to engage Sally Bradford as his servant, his only motive was to remove her from her native Eastbourne where her seduction by an army major had resulted in a child out of wedlock.[29] But she soon becomes his mistress and Neville also resorts to subterfuge to disguise a fact that causes him great anxiety. More feelings of guilt and remorse over (not always) thinly disguised sex with a servant pour from the diaries of Benjamin Smith (1788–1854), a solicitor who lived in Horbling, Lincolnshire. A widower for 13 years, Smith conducted a long-lasting relationship with his maid Mary Newbatt, whom he always referred to by her surname.[30] *"Newbatt came to me this evening and sat with me,"* Smith told his diary – "sat" being his euphemism for sex. Like Rees, Smith is tortured by his secret shame and the effort of keeping up the facade of respectability and gentility: *"May I from this day earnestly resolve to be different and better and correct in my conduct to her! . . . Oh God that I was married . . . May God in his infinite goodness pardon my*

26. Ibid., 23 January 1861.
27. Ibid., 16 January 1862.
28. D. C. Jenkins (editor), *The Diary of Thomas Jenkins of Llandeilo 1826–1870*, Dragon Books, 1976.
29. Basil Cozens-Hardy (editor), *The Diary of Sylas Neville, 1767–1788*, Oxford University Press, 1950.
30. Benjamin Smith, diaries, accounts and papers 1788–1854, Lincolnshire Archives, SMITH 15.

sins." Smith feels guilty when he has sex with her but aches when she does not: *"Newbatt went to bed without coming to me though she knew I wanted her. Oh God I might be well married. Oh God that I was but married to some good woman."* When he eventually gets engaged to a "good woman", Mary Newbatt leaves before the wedding.

Rees Thomas was not lucky enough to meet a good woman. Despite his good intentions, he trudges again and again the road to hell, directed there by his weaknesses, and ending up consumed with guilt and mournful at the disapproval of his relatives and neighbours. Almost everybody is after him and hardly anybody seems to be on his side, except friends like his tenant Evan Griffiths at Dolygrogws and David Lewis, who spends long hours with him poring over legal and financial papers. He is a slave to his family and shows them great patience. He evidently loves his older brother Thomas, but is constantly abused by his children. It doesn't help that he is prepared to take legal action against his own brother, Jenkin, for non-payment of rent on one of the estate's properties, Tyssul Castle, or that he is viewed by his relatives as an over-zealous guardian of his dead brother Thomas's estate. The ruptured family relationships hurt him keenly, but Rees is constantly troubled by his reputation within the wider community. Returning home one time after drinking too much in Llandysul, he falls into the river Teifi as he steps into his coracle, and is mortified at the fact that it happens in full view of a number of onlookers. *"O what a talk there is today about me,"* he tells his diary.[31]

Happily, the underlying mood of mental anguish and despondency is lightened now and then by a lyrical *joie de vivre*. On his way to a fair at Newcastle Emlyn one rainy May morning, for instance, he is struck by the fruit trees, particularly the cherries: *"There are more blossoms on this year than I ever remember before. Every thorn bush is with white garment. O what a beautiful sight to see the buds & blossoms of spring transmuted into flowers and foliage."*[32] At the end of April, 1861, he writes: *"All the cherry, plum & pears are past their full bloom. The trees (cherries) looked beautifully in the meadow last week, the blossoms in clusters & with no leaves."*[33]

Rees is proud of his fruit trees and unforgiving when he sees some lads from Llandysul stealing apples and pears and damaging the branches. He refuses to drop charges against them, and is satisfied when magistrates at Llanfihangel ar Arth impose fines and costs. Not content with one orchard, he plans another and spends a February afternoon planting the new trees. His efforts to improve his inheritance do not go unnoticed. The anonymous writer of his obituary in *The Welshman* newspaper says the Dôl-llan estate was *"in a somewhat dilapidated condition"* when he inherited it. *"But through the industry & skilful management of the deceased it is now made quite an ornament to the locality. Being an experienced farmer himself, he was an ardent promoter of all projects having a tendency to improve the cultivation of the soil, the breeding of animals, and especially the planting and rearing of fruit and other trees, a branch of husbandry in which he excelled."*[34]

The last entry in the diary was 28 August, 1862, and Rees Thomas died 8 November, 1865. His death certificate lists the cause of death as *"neuralgia of the Knee Joint and asthenia from malaria certified."*[35] Death from neuralgia of the knee joint is, of course, laughable, but malaria was not unknown in Britain, although of course Rees may have contracted it on a trip abroad that we know

31. Diary, 11 January 1862.
32. Ibid., 10 May 1860.
33. Diary, 28 April 1861.
34. *The Welshman*, 17 November 1865.
35. Death Certificate dated November 9, 1865.

nothing about. Britain has a long history of malaria, especially in the salt marshes along the coast of southern England and the disease was considered a leading cause of death in many marshland communities 200 years ago, when it was known variously as "marsh fever" or "the ague". Malaria declined progressively from the 1840s onwards, but there were still pockets of the disease in parts of Kent and other low-lying areas of the country in the early 1900s. The last major outbreak occurred in Queenborough on the Isle of Sheppey during World War One after servicemen returning from Macedonia carrying malaria parasites in their blood were billeted on the edge of town. The infection was picked-up by local mosquitoes from the convalescing soldiers and a total of 32 local people were infected over a period of several years. From 1917 to 1952 there were 566 cases of indigenous malaria of which 90% were in or near coastal areas of southeast England. Most of these occurred between 1917 and 1921, after which outbreaks were sporadic with rarely more than two cases reported from an individual county each year. Only 34 cases were reported between 1941 and 1948 and the last known cases of indigenous malaria occurred in London in 1953.[36]

Dr John Cule of Capel Dewi, Llandysul, the leading Welsh medical historian, says it is still possible to transmit – and catch – malaria in Britain: "The temperature is high enough in some summers and there are plenty of mosquitoes. You can catch it from someone who has it via a mosquito – but it's not common and you would be unlucky." Dr Cule says the diagnosis itself in the case of Rees Thomas could be in doubt: "If he had attacks of shivering they might have thought it was malaria, which was common at that time because of the to-ing and fro-ing to India. And if you had a fever it was more romantic to say it was malaria."[37]

Dr Cule also observed that the word *"certified"* only meant that a doctor said it was so: "And at the time we're thinking of, a doctor was regarded as a learned person – but he was not necessarily so." If Rees Thomas did suffer from malaria, it might explain the strange code at the end of each diary entry: he may have been taking constant medication – and that may have multiplied the effects of alcohol.

Further to medical matters, the death certificate of Rees' eldest brother Thomas, who died in February 1860, gives the cause of death as *"dropsy certified"*. Dr Cule says dropsy was very common – oedema is the modern description. It signifies fluid collecting in the lymphatic system but should be regarded as a sign of an illness, not an illness in itself. Descriptions in the diary make it clear that Thomas was indeed suffering oedema, with severe swelling that doctors tried to alleviate by draining off the fluid. Rees tells us that a few days before his brother's last day they drained off an incredible 20 pints. But the diarist talks of other symptoms of his brother's illness: vomiting, abdominal and bowel pain, weakness, fever and fits, delirium and laborious breathing. Dr Cule speculates that Thomas could have been suffering from stomach cancer with secondary cancers affecting his lungs and brain. Dr Cule said: "If he has cancer of the stomach he is going to have all sorts of things associated with it. He would be feeling weak with stomach cancer and vomiting and all of that would alter the fluid balance. There's no doubt that this chap was terminally ill and had lost weight. In many cases of death from stomach cancer there would not be an accurate diagnosis simply because the disease was not so well understood and diagnosis in general was pretty woolly. Just because a doctor said you had cancer of the stomach did not mean you that you did have it – and vice versa."

36. Article by Steve Lindsay and Rob Hutchinson of the School of Biological & Biomedical Sciences, University of Durham, in the Environmental Exchange Institute website climate.org/articles/climate-change-info/death-marshes.
37. Conversation with Dr Cule, 15 January 2011.

8

The Rees Thomas diary is a remarkable record of life in Victorian north Carmarthenshire. The people of Llandysul and the Teifi Valley wander across its pages. There is Gwilym Marles, the poet and teacher to whom his great nephew Dylan Thomas owed his middle name; Dr Henry Harries Davies, who later in the decade came to wider attention as the family doctor in the notorious case of the Fasting Girl of Pencader. Captain Lewes of Llysnewydd makes a brief appearance. Dr David Lloyd, a cousin who is Principal of the Presbyterian Chapel, Carmarthen, brings his family to stay. We meet the Gogerddan Foxhounds and the Bwlchbychan Beagles. We read of an otter trapped and set upon by dogs in the name of sport.

There are also references to customs and traditions particular to rural Wales. Rees records troops of police drafted in to prevent noisy neighbours inflicting the *Ceffyl Pren*, a form of vigilante justice, where a person accused of adultery, domestic violence or an offence against the community would be paraded in person or in effigy through the community on a wooden horse. One old tradition is recorded as coming to an end among the family. When his brother Thomas dies towards the beginning of the diary Rees writes that for the first time the family decides not to uphold the tradition of *gwyliad nos* – staying up all night watching over the corpse until the funeral. And the road to Llanfair is remade with cartloads of stone.

It is parochial, as one would expect for a diary from the early 1860s, but Rees takes us on a trip to London to visit the Great Exhibition – the Great London Exposition held beside the gardens of the Royal Horticultural Society, South Kensington – where he bumps into numerous neighbours from Llandysul and Carmarthen. He visits the Houses of Parliament, the British Museum, Madam Tussauds, the National Gallery, the Crystal Palace, Westminster Abbey and St Paul's Cathedral. He sees "heaps of salmon" in Billingsgate Market and takes a boat up the Thames to Kew Gardens, Back in Llandysul he talks of people in the area hearing the cannons greeting the arrival of Isambard Kingdom Brunel's revolutionary steamship the *Great Eastern* at Milford Haven.

The diary records a different age of farming, where men planted orchards and corn, and women churned butter. It is a historical record as well as an insight into the life of a troubled man. Perhaps, most of all, it punctures the common assumption that life was unremittingly good for a gentleman and landowner. Our more egalitarian perspective tends to picture the Victorian country squire out hunting or dining well, living a comfortable and sophisticated life and waited on by hard pressed and often oppressed servants. It was certainly more comfortable than the lot of the common people, but it was not a life of unbridled luxury and for many, as this diary shows, it was far from lovely. An enterprising freehold farmer lived materially better, and had less to live up to and fewer social duties to perform than the likes of Rees Thomas. As for servants, they were by no means exclusive to the landed classes. Even a tenant farmer on a holding of 80 acres would employ several, as a glance through any contemporary census will confirm.

Some of us may view with disapproval and even disgust the licentiousness and binge drinking of this yeoman farmer 150 years ago. "The record of Pepys's sex life is variously regarded with embarrassment, condemnation or toleration," writes Vincent Brome.[38] And so it will be with some of Rees Thomas's diary. His sexual habits and his binges are character defects that might suggest that he was not a very nice person to know, although the procession of ministers and clergy to his door suggest otherwise. His immediate relatives had little time for him, without realising that no one was perhaps a more severe critic than Rees himself. He despairs of his weaknesses and faults.

---

38. Vincent Brome, *The Other Pepys*, Weidenfeld & Nicolson, 1992.

The anonymous writer of Rees's obituary in *The Welshman* newspaper of 17 November, 1865, saw things differently. He wrote this: *"Cardiganshire – Llandyssil: The untimely removal from the scenes of his labour of Rees Thomas, Esq, of Dolellan, whose lamented death it is our duty to record in our obituary this week, has cast a deep gloom over this town and the surrounding neighbourhood. He was the oldest surviving son of the late David Thomas of Llanfair, and on the death of his father, in 1845, succeeded to the Dolellan estate, then in a somewhat dilapidated condition; but through the industry & skilful management of the deceased it is now made quite an ornament to the locality. Being an experienced farmer himself, he was an ardent promoter of all projects having a tendency to improve the cultivation of the soil, the breeding of animals, and especially the planting and rearing of fruit and other trees, a branch of husbandry in which he excelled. Nor was he less ready, both influentially and pecuniarily [sic], to support all movements towards the advancement and general prosperity of the town and its vicinity. As a neighbour he was not to be surpassed for acts of kindness and benevolence, and as a friend his sterling worth was inestimable. The high estimation in which the deceased gentleman was held was amply proved by the large concourse of people, rich and poor, who, on Tuesday last, accompanied his remains to Pantydefaid Chapel where he was interred in the family burial ground. Requiescat in pace."* We expect obituaries to gloss over the faults and failings of the deceased, but this is unusually sympathetic and very much at odds with the way he thought he was regarded in his community.

As with the life of anyone, dead or alive, there is much we can never know, no matter how revealing what they choose to tell us. An appendix, a Child's Diary written by Rees' nephew David Thomas, gives us other glimpses of the man and his family. From this, and from his own remarkably frank and honest diary, Rees Thomas emerges as a troubled man undone by his human frailties. His diary tells us much about the human condition in general as well as life in the mid Teifi Valley, on the borders of Carmarthenshire and Ceredigion, in the middle years of the 19th century.

Editor's Notes

This diary contains codes and shorthand. For instance the end of each entry is marked with a code. For example: *3 – 3 consistent* or *1 – 2 Idling* or perhaps *"– " unavoidably* or *"– 2 om"*. In addition. a single word – *disgraceful, despairing, remorse,* or, pitifully, *broken-hearted* sometimes closes an entry. There is no way to speculate accurately what the code means; I have retained it only for the first week of the diary, but I have otherwise edited it out – usually, but not always, along with the single word comment. Thomas also uses a code in the body of the diary text for what is unmistakably his sexual behaviour. I left this code intact and tried to render it in print, as accurately as I can from his handwriting, as "com Idt Ls". In instances where he has sex with his servants he barely disguises the name: S't A is his servant Anne, and S't H'h obviously his servant Hannah. Also with his servants he usually records whether he successfully practised *coitus interruptus* by noting "dge" – discharge – either "extlly" (externally) or "intlly", once or twice written in full as internally. In the case of his neighbours I have used the often very broad hints he gives us together with the 1861 census to indicate individuals where possible. These identities are provided in footnotes.

Thomas has "rules" (*r-l-s*) that he reads to himself, often in the woods (*w-ds*) above his home. Similarly when he says he *"Pd in the woods for the first time this year"* (24 January 1860) I assume from that and from other references that he has "prayed" there. I could of course be wrong, but that is my assumption from the context and from my efforts to understand his way of thinking. In most instances I have used square brackets to fill in letters that the diarist omitted. This is done in order to make the manuscript easier to read, but in some significant instances I have retained the original form for illustrative purposes. My motive was always to make the manuscript more readable and accessible while retaining, where possible, authenticity. For the same reason I have corrected some spelling. For instances the diarist is unable to spell "beautiful" or "rabbit", so these are always rendered correctly in order to avoid repetitive intrusions on a reader's attention. But I have left instances like *S't* for "servant", *Sol'r* or similar for "solicitor", *Rev'd* for "Reverend" or *DK* for "drank" or "drunk" because they are easily absorbed and maintain an element of authenticity. Likewise with his use of capital letters. Throughout I have adopted the approach that it would be unnecessarily tedious to retain all the minor mistakes of spelling and grammar.

Thomas makes an entry every single day for the two years and eight months covered by his diary. In his text he uses abbreviated Latin forms for days of the week. These are inconsistent. For instance Sunday can be Sol or Sul. Monday is Lun, Tuesday Mars, Wednesday usually Mer, Thursday Iupt, Jupt or Iov, Friday is Ven and Saturday Satur. Sometimes he prefixes these with Die or simply D. I have changed these to contemporary abbreviations of days of the week in order to increase readability.

Sometimes the entry is limited to the single word *"Int"* or *"Into"*, denoting that he is on one of his not infrequent alcoholic binges. I have edited out some inconsequential or insignificant entries that record, for instance, days spent pouring over account books, getting in the hay or just visiting Llanfair or some other neighbourhood home, although I have retained some of these to illustrate more accurately his life. Similarly I have edited out some references to the weather, while retaining others. The diarist goes to chapel at Pantydefaid nearly every Sunday and visits his solicitor Jones of Gelli-faharan almost every evening as he wrestles with family law suits and wills, but I frequently edited out these references to avoid repetition. On the other hand I have retained some apparently random comments such as *"The goods of Hannah Porth were sold under execution at the suit of Williams Kings Head"* from the entry for 23 January 1862 in case they aid or inform a local historian's research – while editing out, for instance, a reference to an unknown character's big toe being bad.

I have provided three appendices in order to offer a more rounded picture of the people and places of this diary. Appendix One is listed in Pembrokeshire Record Office as A Child's Diary. It was written in 1863 by David Thomas, later better known locally as Captain Thomas of Llanfair, nephew to Rees Thomas and the last of the family to live at Llanfair. The last, undated, section of this intermittent diary appears to be the draft of a legal statement, and refers to an affidavit. The other two appendices outline the histories of Dôl-llan and Llanfair and as far as is known the people who lived there.

I have also tried to research the people Rees mentions in his diary. This has not always been possible, but the results can be found in footnotes and the Biographical Index of People and Characters.

The Diary of Rees Thomas of Dôl-llan 1860–1862

JANUARY 1860

Sunday, January 1st By reflecting upon my Conduct in the last year and & the reckoning of the number of hours spared for mental cultivation, together with the amount spent in consequence of my occasional fits of intemperance also, I find that all my failings and imperfections are entirely attributed to alcoholic drink and to that alone, therefore why is it that I ever taste a single drop of such poison when I plainly see and find that it not merely deprive me of a large amount of money every year but has been heretofore the ruin of morals as well as my character in the eyes of others as I am spoken of in the neighbourhood as a complete Drunkard and that had it not been for that I should have been an useful member of society, therefore I shall henceforth be a t'tler. 1—1 unavoidably.

Mon 2nd The "calenig" day, fine too.[1] Out with the workmen, mother has been unwell for the last four days & today she went to superintend the churning at Tyssil castle[2] & got very ill. Betsy waited upon her all night and Hannah,[3] contrary to my ardent request, went out courting. Weather boisterous and rainy for the last nine days. 2—4 confirmable.

Tues 3rd Brother Thomas[4] here to dinner, accompanied him to Mr Jones office,[5] had some business there myself for mother, Thomas is drinking spirituous liquors so soon after suffering so severely at the last attack of illness. Today he was not able to mount his horse without having steps. [added later] This was the last time he went from home. 1—1 unavoidably.

Wednes 4th At house making my accounts. It is reported that Mrs Jones Gelliffaren[6] is drinking the contents of my brother Thomas's will which was made by her son. Br[7] Jenkin & the two little girls of Llanfair here.[8] 2—2 unavoidably.

---

1. *Calenig* – children's custom of collecting gifts on New Year's Day by going door to door reciting a traditional rhyme. The previous day, being a Sunday, was obviously unsuitable in the strictly Sabbath-respecting society of Victorian Wales.
2. Tyssil Castle, a small mansion and estate overlooking the bridge at Llandyssul, now known as Caer-y-Glyn.
3. Betsy & Hannah are Dôl-llan servants.
4. Thomas Thomas, Rees's eldest brother.
5. John Jones (1834–1884), Gelli Faharen, was the Thomas family solicitor.
6. John Jones's mother, Jane Jones, whose grandfather was Dafydd Davis of Castell Hywel. The Jones family was therefore related to Rees Thomas. [H. R. Evans, 'A Village Worthy', *Ceredigion*, Vol. IV, No. 2, 1961.]
7. Br = "brother", a shorthand used throughout the diary.
8. Jenkin Thomas, also known as Jenkyn Jones Thomas, a younger brother. The two little girls of Llanfair were Rees's nieces Mary and Anne or Annie, eldest daughters of Thomas Thomas.

Thurs 5th Br David[9] received other form from my solicitor stating that an executor will come out to arrest him tomorrow or Saturday for the sum including cost above £20 – that sum before costs was only £8 at first. The amount of costs was incurred in consequence of Br Thomas's delaying to pay but stated to me this long time that he had discharged that debt and today found otherwise. He, Thomas, is ailing this week again. The doctor was sent for yesterday & obliged to use the catheter as pain and swelling were increasing. 2—4 consistent.

Fri 6th At Tyssil castle by six this morning with £20 to Jenkin to go to Carmarthen to discharge Tom Parry's claim.[10] He immediately went. Br Evan[11] sent his servant with a letter here last night desiring mother to send him a pair blankets, three persons to plant fir trees and the loan of ten pounds. The only answer sent by mother to him was that as long as he employed Jones Vronwen about the fir for him not to send to her for anything and I told that servant to tell Evan that the first time that I should see him here I would give him a good strong horse whip over his back. That rascal Jones stayed two or three days at Nantegryd with the view of having to give him a written contract about his orders and it seems that it succeeded in his dishonest design though Jenkin advised him to the contrary. 1 3 4 unavoidably.

Sat 7th Planting fruit trees in new orchard in Cae Susern. Br T[12] ailing very bad at night. Dr Davis sent for.[13] 1/ twice.

Mon 9th Planting fruit trees this fine day. Servant Betsy is very good since Martha left. She is really very economical in all things. Servant Hannah is very negligent, dirty & lazy and too much of a talker to work out.

Tues 10th I was called over to Llanfair. My brother was very ill. There all day. Dr Phillips of Newcastle was sent for but was not home. Thomas was pretty good all day but had a fit at noon & since then he got bad and continued so all night. I was there all the time until this morning the 11th. Yet there is a large quantity of water in his abdomen. The fits he gets arises [*sic*] from shortness of breath. Thomas when in a fit calls for Jenkin & myself always. Poor fellow, he is an object to be highly pitied. Dr Davis's opinion of him tonight was that he may linger for years yet that he may die in an hour when in a fit.

Thurs 12th Old Christmas day.[14] To Llanfair at am. At home till 4 o'clock pm then over to the village about preparing the books & bills to be entered tomorrow in the County Court. Jenkin is entered at the suit of Twm Elias for an old horse for the dogs about five years ago, the price was only 10/-. Br Evan is entered by uncle Ffoshelig & Danny his old servant by the former for £10

---

9. David Thomas, another younger brother, who was mentally unstable.
10. The debt referred to in the previous day's entry.
11. Of Nantegryd, Rees's youngest brother.
12. Brother Thomas.
13. Dr Henry Harries Davies, born 1836, in practice in Llandysul from *c*.1858. [See Harold Selcon, *The Changing Face of Medicine in 20th Century Llandysul*, Llandysul Local History Society, 2003, pp. 4-7.]
14. *Calan Hen*, refers to the 11 days "lost" in 1752 when the calendar was changed from the Old Style (Julian) system to the New Style (Gregorian) calculation. The custom of marking *Calan Hen* has continued to the present day in Llandysul.

and the latter about £11.[15] It is really shameful for them both, Jenkin and Evan. One is as bad as the other. Had a very long conversation with Jones solicitor on his way home & among other things he advised me to refuse being named as an executor to the will of Br Thomas.

Fri 13th Finishing planting fruit trees. Dr Phillips visited Br T this afternoon and pronounced him convalescent & almost out of danger. Stayed myself there for an half hour. Had many messages for him [to] take at Carmarthen tomorrow. One thing is to ask for a copy of the will of the late Mr Jenkin Beynon Llaethlyw.[16]

Sat 14th To Carmarthen to pay Parry's solicitor's bill against my Br David. It amounts to £22-4-2. I left his bill & the amount in the hands of Mr Lewis Morris[17] solicitor to pay him. He (Lewis Morris) very kindly came with me from his own office to that of Parry twice in order to prevail upon Parry to make some abatement in his exorbitant bill. I have been asked for a copy of the late Mr Jenkin Beynon's will, paid £1.0.6 for a copy. Been very moderate in drinking only one glass of Beer & that one I could not refuse to take. Br Thomas had a fit last night yet he is better today.

Sun 15th To Llanfair at pm, remained there till late. Br Thomas is just the same, down in the kitchen and as talkative as ever. His legs were [a] little swollen. Jenkin there. Jenkin is, though unwell, smokes a good deal, also takes a tiff now & then of anything that he can secretly have.

Mon 16th Rent audit day of Llanfair estate. I was asked by brother to receive them and so did, & to his satisfaction I think. The quibbling & grumbling by some were truly very unpleasant & had I known of it beforehand I would not have gone there at all, so do not on any account whatever receive them again. Heavy shower & very dark when we (E. Griffiths) were coming home, crossed in the coracle. Quite exhausted.

Tues 17th Arranging the rent account book of Llanfair here, failed to have the figures in the book & the amount received to correspond within 18/-. Terrible unnecessary trouble brought on myself without any interest to me personally. Over to Llanfair in the evening with the said book & a copy of the will of the late JB of Llaithlyw. The Rev'd T. Thomas Pantydefaid[18] was there. Br became very ill indeed and at his request remained with him all night. The water in the abdomen is still on the increase & he cannot turn in bed without assistance & is now taking more than the allowance of

---

15. Uncle Ffoshelig – The Tithe Map of 1841 has another Rees Thomas as owner-occupier of Ffoshelyg. He was the brother of Rees's father David. This entry shows how close members of the family were ready to litigate over debts.
16. Jenkin Beynon was the uncle of Mary, deceased wife of Rees's brother Thomas, and extremely rich. He owned most of Llangrannog and lived at Llaethlliw, two miles south-east of Aberaeron. Evans died in 1849 and the will, which left legacies to support local two schools as well as sums of money to members of the Thomas family, was the subject of a protracted case in Chancery that dragged on until 1870.
17. Lewis Edward William Morris (1797–1872) of Mount Pleasant, later Penbryn, Llangunnor, father of the poet and author Lewis Morris. [See Francis Jones, *Historic Carmarthenshire Homes and Their Families*, p. 146.]
18. Rev'd Thomas Thomas (no relation), Minister of Pantydefaid Unitarian Chapel, Prengwyn, since 1847. The Thomas family had a close connection with the chapel, having been instrumental in securing a burial ground for the church and having endowed two stained glass windows. [See D. Elwyn Davies, *They Thought for Themselves*, J. D. Lewis and Sons Ltd., Gomer, Llandysul, 1982, pp. 44-46.]

gin. His servant Ann is the most active and attentive girl I ever saw & undoubtedly she richly deserves a most handsome present.[19] Drank a glass of wine & one of Beer.

Wednes 18th Came home from Llanfair about 8 o'clock this morning. Returned again in order to settle with some of his creditors. Paid Jones Vronwen £30 & there is balance again to him, £17.7.6d. All this amount for fir planted last year at Vrongoch & Gwtheyrn. Poor Thomas was taken in of at least £35.0.0.

Thurs 19th To Llanfair this morning. Br had an awful night the last. It seems that he had excruciating pain in his bowels & his breathing was short and difficult. Today he was apparently pretty well, talking & chatting & laughing. The swelling increases & is now pronounced by Dr Phillips in danger as veins must be had to tapping. Dr Davis never comes there after he had a bottle of medicine from Dr Phillips. What a proud & haughty fellow Davis is.

Sat 21st Left Llanfair about seven this morning, took a glass of brandy when leaving & it took a very great effect on me. The wind blew my coracle into the river. My brother was from 11 o'clock to 3 this morning extremely poorly, groaning very loud at times & sometimes apparently dead, mouth open, insensible & very pale. Also he was pretty delirious, thinking and desiring to be taken to the top of a mountain, & he was gasping for breath. Mother, Jenkin & myself were down with him. It was truly very hard to look at him. Dr Phillips visited him today & pronounced him in very dangerous state & must be tapped on Monday.

Sun 22nd Mr Evans Court Farm[20] was in Llandyssul yesterday all day & he came not to see my brother. He sent his servant girl to ask how he was today & he is better too.

Mon 23rd Down to Llanfair attending my brother all night. He had an excellent night, no pain or difficulty breathing, but sound asleep all night. Today he was little worse and was in great anxiety for seeing Dr Phillips, from whom he had not heard all day. He stated that he will be a teetotaller for the remainder of his life & that his conduct shall undergo a complete change of course for the better.

Tues 24th Dr Davis has been parading the village yesterday & today half drunk. Dr Phillips, as I met him coming from Llanfair, pronounced Thomas convalescent & as he said, "He will get round it without having recourse to tapping." Pd [prayed?] in the woods the first time this year.[21]

Wednes 25th To Llanfair at pm to wait upon Thomas over the night. He was suffering much from pain in the bowels after one o'clock in the morning to seven. I was informed there that the Rev'd Evan Evans Llaethlyw[22] was married yesterday & most unfortunately it is likely to be too true. I myself feel disappointed somehow or other.

---

19. The first reference to Ann Thomas, then aged 22 or 23, who he later hires as his house maid.
20. John Evans of Court Farm, Cwrtnewydd. He married Anne, sister of Jenkin Beynon. Their daughter, Mary, married Rees' brother Thomas. Rees is disgusted that Evans did not call to see his sick son-in-law while he was in Llandysul.
21. From the context of this and other similar references, Rees is in the habit of praying in the woods, probably the ancient woodland of Allt Dôl-llan that still overlooks Llandysul.
22. The Rev'd Evan Evans, Llaethllyw (Llaethlliw), second (and surviving) son of John Evans.

Thurs 26th Thomas has suffered much pain during the night. Ann Lewis Nantegryd[23] here over last night. Evan has been abusing her very much & sent for Montalembert[24] to make her account & to pay her. She left here this morning again to fetch her clothes from Nantegryd so I have not seen her afterwards. Made a new coracle as the one that was made about a fortnight ago was blown in the river & cut up. Mother has almost completely recovered from her cold. Is very whimsical and obstinate in everything that will be of any good to her. It was impossible for her to live long. About her accounts all day.

Mon 30th With my brother Thomas all last night. It seems that he is offended with me for something or other, probably that Jenkin or his children has [sic] said something on me that may provoke offence as both are very double facedness. Jenkin is prevailing upon him to change some clauses in his will & probably the executor & really I should be very glad of getting rid of the executorship.

FEBRUARY 1860

Wednes 1st To Llanfair all last night. Dr Jones[25] was there almost all night. Dr Phillips came up about 8 o'clock this morning. They tapped my brother. Twenty pints of water ran out. He became for the remainder of the day much better.

Fri 3rd At home unwell partly from Drink & bad cold. Remained in the house all day. Took some pills of Dr Jones. Pain in my chest & side & very nervous, Br T it seems is not much better. My Drink fever is nibbed [sic] in the bud this time. However the sooner the better to return to total abstinence.

Sat 4th Thomas not much the worse. Water was fast dripping from the hole made for tapping. Dr Phillips and Jones visited him today & pronounced him in much danger. Thomas's creditors are raining upon him for paying their debts. The current report is that he is over head & ears in debt, also that we will pay. Also I expect that my creditors will come upon me immediately. The creditors of David & Evan are pouncing upon them. God knows what we can do. The former report that we were wealthy is now at an end. O how have we reduced ourselves in the eyes of the world. I am truly bewildered from what I have heard with Jones solicitor tonight about us. He is going to Llanfair on Monday to tell Thomas how he instructed him about his creditors.

Sun 5th Thomas is getting weaker. Poor fellow, he gives mournful hyms [sic] out when in bed & then he sings there himself with a mournful tone & sometimes desires us to join him. He sings now much better than when he was well. It is truly heartrending to hear him. Some[thing] of which I know not yet has caused him to offend with me. Mother is not allowing any stranger to be down with him at night & she is very peevish & whimsical to all around. As soon as I came to understand that I have offended the sick I have not afterwards been there with him at night, nor since made but a very short stay when I go there.

23. One of the servants of Rees's brother Evan.
24. Montalembert – apparently an agent or solicitor.
25. Dr John Jones of Tyssul Lodge, practiced in Llandysul from c.1851, died 1879 aged 69. Ibid., Selcon.

Mon 6th I went over to the office of Jones who, as he told me, sent his clerk to Llanfair with a letter demanding immediate payment of £700 down from my brother Thomas to John Davis Peny-pistill, one of the Irish. Stated to Jones that that proceedings of his (considering the precarious state in which my brother was) will not soon be forgotten. John Rees Bwlchyronen has given his bond of £237 down from my brother Thomas to him to John Jones in order to take immediate proceedings to recover the sum. However in order to calm the talk of my brother's debts & to stop legal proceedings against my poor brother, who is most likely on his death bed, I promised to give an undertaking that I should be responsible for his debts myself.

Tues 7th I was called at half past 12 last night to go up immediately to Nantegryd as Br Evan was very ill. After I went up he was in bed labouring under Delirium Tremens accompanied with spasms of vomiting till he was apparently dead. Dr Davis remained there all night. Today he is much better. Spasms have almost left him. From Nantegryd this morning to Llanfair. Poor Br Thomas fast sinking. Drs Phillips and Jones pronounced him today to be in a dying state. The former stated that it would be of no avail to give him any more medicines as that he could not live more than two days. He groaned [a] good deal at times today and discontinued singing & repeating hymns yesterday. Jones's solicitors clerk went to Llanfair this afternoon with two letters and the contents of them were well worthy of the cruel heart of Nero, the following a verbatim copy of each.[26]

Wednes 8th Came home from Llanfair about 8 o'clock this morning, been there all night. Poor Thomas was very restless till he had a draught to calm him this morning about 2 o'clock. He groaning loud and frequent until that time, moving constantly either from the bed to the easy chair or from the latter back. Water was freely running from the hole where he was tapped. He knew everyone but he was too weak to speak. Many a time he called for his late wife. Truly it was heartrending to hear him at a distance but cannot be described how hard to be with him. Br Evan is come once more to his senses & likely out of danger.

Thurs 9th Came home from Llanfair this morning. Been to Nantegryd last night for informing Br Evan of the true state of poor Br T. Yesterday Dr Jones stated that Thomas would expire before 12 o'clock today. However he is yet alive, though like as if dead, eyes half open, mouth quite so, breathing quite easy & the intervals between each breath is double longer than that of a healthy person. No words were uttered once yesterday & when spasm comes on which lasts from up to 2 hours he then poor fellow is suffering the most excruciating pain & is calling out yesterday & today on his late wife.[27] "Mary Mary fach dewch yma." Mary again twice, then it follows by either of these words, Dewch yma; Ble yr ich I; Tymma fi,[28] & he (is) generally begins by calling 2 or 3 times Man Man fach, & then his wife during the whole attack of spasm. Indeed it was truly heartrending to see him. He is calling so loud that I can hear him when the doors of the house are closed for 200

---

26. Unfortunately, the copies are missing. There is a blank page in diary at this point, followed by a page of scribbled sums and accounts, the only intelligible one is transcribed as follows:
    Room[?] 6/-; coals 1/-; meat 4/-; Bread 9d; Butter 8d; Vegetables 6d; Tea 6d; Sugar 2½d; Sundries[?] 1/-; Milk 3½d; washing[?] 6d; oil 3d; Total 16/8d [*sic*; total = 15/8d].
27. Mary Thomas, neé Evans, died 2 July 1856, aged 40, soon after giving birth to her fifth child.
28. Welsh translation – "Mary Mary dear, come here. Come here. Where are you I'm here."

yards from Pistyll. When he took the "anodyne" draught he falls asleep & will remain in that state from 8 to 9 hours and as soon as he awakens he begins calling very loudly out. Dr Jones very kindly attends him ever.

Fri 10th At Llanfair all last night. Br T awake at 9 o'clock last night & immediately began calling very loudly out, Oh Dir [sic], & continued in that state till half past four this morning. His voice was as strong & as clear as ever had been except his arms was [sic] quite motionless. The "anodyne" draught was not given to him (as Dr Jones desired) before 4 o'clock this morning. No words, or at least very few, were uttered by him now for many days past. Yet he knows some of us that attend him & he stares in a person's face when he asks him anything & will either give an answer (quite unaudible [sic]) or little shake of his head. The sign when he wishes to have something to drink is putting his tongue out.

Sat 11th To Llanfair after breakfast this morning. I went up as soon as I went there to see my dear brother Thomas and found him taking his last breath. His mouth was quite open & his eyes closed. I left his room immediately as it was too hard for me to stand & in about 15 minutes he expired. By this time it was half past 9 o'clock am when he died. He is exceedingly calm & easy from 8 o'clock the previous night. The last anodyne draught was given to him that time. He awoke about 1 o'clock in the morning & groaned a little in a feeble tone of voice & from that time to his departure he was fast sinking and never uttered a single word. Poor brother. How happy should I be to see him walking out once more over his lands & to have a few words with him once more.[29]

Sun 12th To Llanfair early this morning. The shell[30] was made ready by 2 o'clock this morning & the corpse was put in it & taken down to the drawing room. Old Evans of Court Farm was there.[31] No one is to remain in the room with the corpse & only one or two strangers[32] is allowed to be there over the night. Two of the domesticks [sic] & the stranger are down in the kitchen every night. We agreed to discontinue the old fashion of Gwilad y corpse in the same room with him.[33] Now the room is locked with two candles burning therein at each end of the shell. Mother & Jenkin are there day and night. The children[34] wishes [sic] Jenkin to come there immediately to live that no change may be made at Llanfair.

Mon 13th To Llanfair for three hours today. Mother, Jenkin & the children appear rather sulky to me, for what cause I am at a loss to know. My cart took some wood, lime and 27 Carnarvon [sic] slates up for the grave, Jenkin's cart two loads of stone and Llanfair's one load of Flags from the Kennel for the same purpose.

---

29. "On the 11th instant aged 43 years Thomas Thomas Esq of Llanfair, Llandyssul, Cardiganshire. Deceased was much respected by a large circle of acquaintance, and his death is regretted especially by his young family of five children who are left orphans to deplore their irreplaceable loss." – Notice in the *Carmarthen Journal* probably inserted by Rees.
30. Coffin.
31. "Old Evans = John Evans of Cwrt Farm, Llanwenog, father-in-law of the dead man.
32. Strangers. This may refer to the practice of "sin-eating". [See Trefor M. Owen, *Welsh Folk Customs*, National Museum of Wales, Welsh Folk Museum, Cardiff, 1959.]
33. *Gwilad y corpse* – the custom of sitting up all night with the dead body.
34. Thomas Thomas had five children, Ann then aged 15, David, 12, Mary, 11, John, 7, and Jane 4.

Tues 14th To Llanfair this morning and remained there almost all day. Watty[35] & others are repairing the civin [civil?] road which is in a very bad state.[36] Searched some of the papers of my late brother among which found an IOU from E. Evans Llaithliw to my late brother for £1,000. David is drinking at an average for the last month more than a quart of spirituous liquor a day.

Wednes 15th To Llanfair repairing the roads & other things preparatory to the funeral. Rev'd E. Evans Llaithliw come there at dusk very drunk.

Thurs 16th Today was the funeral of a kind and generous brother & deeply we lamented his loss. He wished many a time upon me to allow myself to be named & to act as an executor & so I could not refuse. The funeral was very large & the day was fine and thawing. The coffin was closed tight and it was a day that proved hard upon my feelings. I could not go to Llanfair without my feelings being much affected by the thought that my dear brother is no more, seeing what a fine place he has made of it, & as soon as he had completed the great improvements there was summoned by the cold hand of death to quit it for ever. Rev'd E. Evans Llaithliw came to the funeral in a very drunken state, could hardly stand on his feet. O what an awful spectacle. He fell asleep at Panty-defaid Chapel & had not been awakened by anybody until the corpse was lowered into the grave & the flags put over it. David Carp't Ffynnonbwla[37] was also very drunk at the funeral & noticed by all. Mr David Thomas Rhydowen was the undertaker & a righteous man he is. Mr Evans Court & his son went home from Pantydefaid but not before the burial. Br Evan accompanied the funeral to the chapel & then went home as he was very nervous & poorly though quite sober but in great grief after the only brother that used to pay him an almost diurnal visit.

Fri 17th To Llanfair all day, took paper from there and arranging thing about there. Sishi,[38] David & Jenkin & Evan there. David was sent for to Llanfair the day before the funeral & is there still, he had not been at the funeral as we were afraid that he would not conduct himself properly.

Sat 18th At Llanfair all day from early in the morning. Evan Griffiths Dolygrogwys came with me all over the land. Jenkin & the children were at Nantegryd all day, very active indeed & not conducting myself with the utmost propriety. Hope God will continue to assist me. Took all the papers of my late brother over with me in order to arrange them here. My poor brother's papers & account are in a sad state.

Sun 19th At home in the House all day. Very bad cold, sneezing & coughing constantly. Betsy gave me most unwarrantable abusive language for only preventing to put too large a lumps [sic] of coal on the fire. I have told her not to do so scores of times before. She abuses us all as a family when in a rage & tried even my late departed brother.

---

35. Watty: Walter James, 38, Dôl-llan farm servant and tenant of Dôl-llan Lodge, where he lived with his wife Anne, 37. [*1861 Census, Llanfihangel ar Arth.*]
36. It was customary to repair the road before a funeral.
37. David Titus, 40, carpenter. Lived at Ffynnonbwla with his Rachel, 39 and their children, son David, 17 and daughters Dinah, 13; Sarah, 9, Elizabeth, 4. [*1861 Census, Llanfihangel ar Arth.*]
38. Rees's sister Margaret, married to John Davies.

Mon 20th At Llanfair all day arranging papers and other things. Extremely cold, heavy showers of snow accompanied by high wind. Br Jenkin states that he greatly desires to be Trustee in lieu of Mr Jones Llwyngroes[39] who he says that he will not act, at least Jenkin wishes him to resign. I am perfectly willing to resign everything that I have in connection with the will but Jenkin refuses to take it.

Tues 21st To Llanfair this morning to meet Mr Evans Court Farm who came there about 11 o'clock in order as I desired him to have his opinion [of] the affairs then. We are of the opinion that to make a sale there next September and to let the land out in fields by auction will be best. Accompanied him to Nantegryd in order to ask William old serv't of Llanfair to come there till the sale but he refused. Deep snow and great drifts.

Wednes 22nd In the evening went to Jones's office as he requested about £700 of Penpistill. He therefore stated that he would not delay for a single day in serving me (as an executor) with a writ of summons to recover the sum. After begging him to delay till the next Saturday before giving costs but refused a day for me & at last told him to take his course & that the money would be paid tomorrow evening so I must by all means endeavour to get them from the Bank Carmarthen tomorrow.

Thurs 23rd To Carmarthen with the copy of the will of my late brother & asking the loan of £700 to pay John Davis Penpistill. Money refused in Morris Bank on any account. However had a promise for them at Wilkins Bank by Mr Lewis Morris, Mother & myself jointly giving a note for the amount & for me to deposit the conveyance Deed of Dolellan as an additional security for them, which was not with me in Town today so had to return home without the money & in a very low spirits.

Fri 24th To Carmarthen this morning with the conveyance deed of Dolellan & my mother's signature in a note payable two months after the date for the value of £520.

Sat 25th To John Jones's office with the money to pay John Davis Penpistill Bond for £700 & interest thereon from the 16th last December. Jones not come. Offered through his clerk, but refused, stating that two writs of summonses were coming by the post today in order to serve me with one for the amount of Penpistill & the other for the recovery of the Bond of John Rees Gwastod for £250 & interest thereon for the year. Hasten to meet the little lawyer to Abercerdyn & then after waiting him for half an hour he came & was very proud and haughty & after begging of him to receive the Penpistill amount then, which he last condescended by me handing him £10 to recover the interest & the two writs which he never told me that I was to be served with.

Sun 26th I am informed that the Bailiffs have taken possession of all the personals of the Rev'd Evan Evans Llaithliw & the most part of his creditors will have no dividend whatever. Mother is in much trouble about her £2,000. My late brother has given his name with him for about £5,000, which probably his estate will have to pay.

The next three days, and much of the next month are taken up with dealing with paperwork relating to Llanfair, debts and legal matters.

---

39. William Jones, aged 32, Squire of Llwyngroes, Llanwnnen, landowner and magistrate and farmer of 150 acres. [*1861 Census, Llanwnen*; Francis Jones, *Historic Cardiganshire Homes and their Families*, Brawdy Books, 2000.]

MARCH 1860

Thurs 1st At home with Evan Evans Nantcoch[40] arranging papers of our lately deceased brother.

Mon 5th Little David and his sister Anne[41] are very angry with me, the former for desiring him to prepare a lessons [sic] in some book for me to teach him & the latter for saying that she was to go to school again. Great pain in my bowels.

Tues 6th To Llandyssil, Llanfair & the remainder of the day with Evans Nantcoch, arrange papers, him very active all day & what an encouragement when finding the children of Llanfair are so desperate against me & as so to their own interest. Betsy in a perpetual rage.

Wednes 7th Mother was served yesterday by Jacky John from the County Court sent to Jones solicitor to make approvance [sic] against him for the amount, which is £3.17.4. After I came home from Carmarthen a letter had come from Mr Jenkins solicitor Cardigan stating that proceedings was [sic] to be taken by him for £400 due from Evans Llaithliw & my late brother. Br Evan was at Carmarthen with a fat bullock to be sold. The beast became frightened and furious & poor Evan drunk & foolish. It was sold at 4.30pm. It was a reduced price to what was offered in the morning for him and it would not have been sold for any price had Evan not fallen asleep. But it was more judicious to sell him at almost any price that [sic] to bring him home as the expense in brandy alone was enormous.

Fri 9th To Newcastle Emlyn. Intox.[42]

Mon 12th Bewildered.

Tues 13th Dreadful remorse. Been to Llanfair at am & to Mr Jones office at pm respecting Mother's bill's affairs particularly Jacky John. I am almost driven to a hopeless state by all the trouble I have in my capacity as an executor & my brother David's affairs, also my mother's as well.

Wednes 14th To Llanfair. Servant Betsy is as stupid to everything I ask of her as if she was a piece of stone. After I came home tired and exhausted and asking for victuals of her they will not be given till she will first finish all her previous work. Never have I heard or seen [a] wife treating her husband as my Servant treats me; if a midling [sic] Welsh girl could be had B would be dismissed from my service instantly.

Thurs 15th Mother kindly gave me a fowl & some veal as Betsy refused to prepare anything for the Rev'd T. Evans[43] tomorrow.

---

40. A watchmaker and engraver who continually helps Rees with his work.
41. David Thomas, born 10 October 1848 and Anne (Annie) Thomas, born 15 May 1845, children of Rees' recently deceased brother Thomas.
42. Intoxicated – the first of many of Rees's binges. This one lasted for three days.
43. The Rev'd Titus Evans, Unitarian Minister and school teacher.

Fri 16th Sent a cart to Stag and Pheasant[44] to meet the Rev'd T. Evans. He arrived late in the evening in order to arrange & examine the Title deed of Llanfair, which I brought over today. Preparing evidence to disprove the items of Jacky John's bill against Mother at the next County Court next Friday.

Sat 17th To Carmarthen. Mr Lloyd Davis[45] is very very ill. Rev'd T. Evans here last night examining & arranging the Title deeds of Llanfair. Mr R. Thomas Cribor was in town relative to the writ he served on Evans Llaithliw.

Mon 19th Mr Lloyd Davis is almost in a hopeless state to recover. The only talk about the county for the last month is about the liabilities of the Llanfair & Llaithliw estates, the liabilities of the latter stated above £25,000 & really it is not much above the mark.

Tues 20th To Jones office for Mother's affairs. To Cerrig Cefen, Llanfair to stop the fox holes as the Gogerddan hounds have promised me to come and hunt there tomorrow.[46] Br Evan brought a yard or more of hay here today. A very strange thing took place here last night. That was, Mother came and slept in this house last night, which she did not for at least 8 years or more before. It was caused from fear to sleep in her own house.

Wednes 21st Went to meet with Evan Evans Pistill to meet Gogerddan fox hounds to Bwlch-bychan[47] but before we reached there they had met them coming down towards Waunifor in full cry so we followed them to Cwmnant where the fox was lost & we turned home.

Thurs 22nd The County Court is to be held tomorrow and I am in great fear that Jacky John will not give in before. Not a moment can be spared for reading now. Mr Lloyd Davis Blaendyffryn died about 7 o'clock yesterday morning & undoubtedly many will have a severe loss in his wise advice as he was everything in this part, yes, quite an useful man to society.[48] My own loss will be very great.

Fri 23rd To Newcastle [Emlyn] about Mother's affairs, especially Jacky John, who has taken legal proceedings against her as executor of my late brother John for the recovery of £3.17.9 due as he asserted for work. Thomas had no chance of opposing him with success on account of the terrible bad state of his (John's) accounts, in fact he had no account at all, therefore I was obliged to give in. So Jones my solicitor settled with him by paying him £2.0.0 before entering the court. I had five defaulters against whom I entered proceedings. They all paid before today. The masons this

---

44. Stag and Pheasant at Pontarsais, about halfway to Carmarthen.
45. John Lloyd Davies (1801–1860) of Blaendyffryn and Alltrodyn.
46. Gogerddan Hounds – Sir Pryse Pryse of Gogerddan (1838–1906) lived for hunting – and died for it, within one week of being bitten by a fox at the age of 68 in 1906.
47. Bwlchbychan, Llanwenog, part of the Gogerddan estate and occupied by John Pugh Vaughan Pryse (1818–1903), third son of Pryse (Loveden) Pryse of Gogerddan, Llanbadarn Fawr. He hunted as often as he could. [See Herbert Vaughan, *The South Wales Squires*, Methuen & Co., 1926.
48. "On 21st Instant at Blaendyffryn, Cardiganshire, in the 59th year of his age, John Lloyd Davies Esq, magistrate and Deputy Lieutenant of the counties of Carmarthen and Cardigan and late MP for Carmarthen Borough." *Carmarthen Journal*, 23 March 1860.

week commenced erecting a little house down in the corner of Pencastle Garden. Drank 4 glasses of Br so got quite stupid.

Sun 25th At home all day as unwell (little). At noon consequently drank two wine glasses of Gin & then got quite stupid for the remainder of the day. Capt Lewis Llysnewydd[49] very kindly sent me (as promised last week at Newcastle Emlyn) the Country Gentlemen's Magazine, being a weekly paper principally treating on agriculture, published in Dublin. He promised to send it occasionally.

Thurs 29th To Llanfair at am. Ffair blodau day.[50] At home the remainder of the day & I am sorry when I report that I wasted it without making progress.

Sat 31st March is gone, little good made of it, yet I must recollect that not much time I had to spare for reading as the duties that devolved upon me as an executor takes two-thirds of my time. Never I think or can recollect that my Sexual inclin'ts had been so strong as in the closing month but I think I have not yet this year com Idt Ls.[51]

APRIL 1860

Sun 1st Reading at am, chapel at pm. Brother & Anne Thomas were there. Went before me all the way home. They are both it seems highly indignant with me and little shall I care as long as I will give them no real cause. Very little reading religious books today. Drank all the Beer.

Fri 6th To Llanfair this morning in order to advance Jenkin the money for the school of the children who are leaving him tomorrow morning. Mother & Sister have been here yesterday. The former was in a bad temper to me for what cause I do not know, yet she was very kind to sister and gave her £5. Anne my niece says that she will never ask nor come near me for any money.

Wednes 11th Dr Davis married Miss Louisa James today and undoubtedly he had the best lady for a good wife that Llandyssil can bred & born.[52] I [am] almost certain that she will make an excellent wife. The bells pealed on the occasion for about two hours. I am since yesterday suffering the most intolerable Ictg. O what can alleviate such thing. My mind wandered, yes drunk constantly on the abuse of the 12 since the beginning of March. Never in my life I have been the like before.[53]

---

49. Captain William Price Lewes, Llysnewydd, Llangeler (1813–1890). Old gentry family, also owned Llanerchaeron, near Aberaeron and Duffryn, Llandybie. High Sheriff of Carmarthenshire in 1860. Annual income of between £4,000 and £5,000.
50. *Ffair Blodau*, a livestock fair held the Thursday before Palm Sunday at Llandysul since at least the 16th century.
51. An example here of the code Rees used to write about sex or sometimes lascivious thoughts. He writes a phrase most readily transcribed in print as something like "com Idt Ls".
52. Dr Henry Harries Davies married Louisa James, daughter of the Rev'd Evan James, Vicar of Llandysul and the man who replaced the riotous football match at *Calan Hen* with a religious festival that survives to the present day. Louisa and their only child Charlotte, were dead within five years – ibid., Harold Selcon.
53. This code and diary entry may relate to temptation of some kind. Rees refers to "Ictg" [itching?] and "the abuse of the 12" on several occasions. He appears to have 12 commandments or rules.

Llandyssil 1813, edited image of print showing Dôl-llan and the church.

Dôl-llan, 2004.
(Photograph: Steve Dubé).

Rees Thomas diary cover.
(Photograph: Steve Dubé, courtesy of Pembroke Record Office).

Thomas family coat of arms.
(Photograph: Steve Dubé).

*Dôl-llan house portrait on stairs of
unknown Victorian man (house
owner says it was there when
they came – is it Rees Thomas?).*
(Photograph: Steve Dubé).

Rees Thomas, signature.
(Photograph: Steve Dubé).

RHYS THOMAS m GWENLLIAN   daughter of John Evans, Gwarcoed Einion, Llandysul

Llanfair & Ffosesgob

THOMAS THOMAS m (1) JANE   dtr of Rev David Lloyd, Llwynrhydowen & Brynllefrith

Llanfair   (2) Anne David

DAVID THOMAS m MARY dtr of John & Susannah Edwards   Rev. Thomas Thomas   Rees Thomas   JENKIN BEYNON   ANNE BEYNON   d1845
1784-1845   1785-1874   of Wernmacwydd   1779-1818   Ffoshelig   1778-1849   m JOHN EVANS
Llanfihangel ar Arth   Cwrt Farm,

THOMAS m MARY   David Beynon Evans   Rev. EVAN EVANS
1817-60   1815-56   1817-55   1820-63

MARGARET   John   REES THOMAS   DAVID   JENKIN   EVAN
1814-92   1819-58   1823-65   1825-76   1828-80   1830-64

m Rev. Thomas Howell Davies, Rector of Llangunllo

GRACE   ANNE (Susanna Gwenllian)   FRANCES   LOUISA   MARY   JANE   DAVID   JOHNNY   ?

DAVID   MARY   JOHN   JANE   ANNE
1846-82   1848-68   1852-70   1856   1845-94

Thomas family tree.
(Compiled by Steve Dubé).

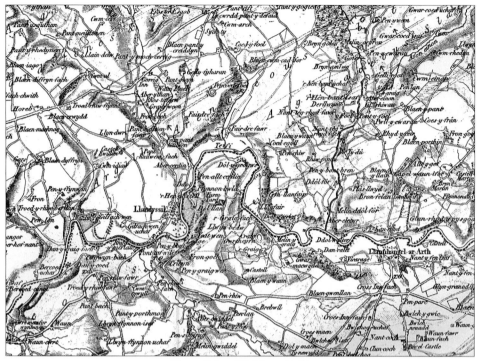

First edition OS Map, 1865.

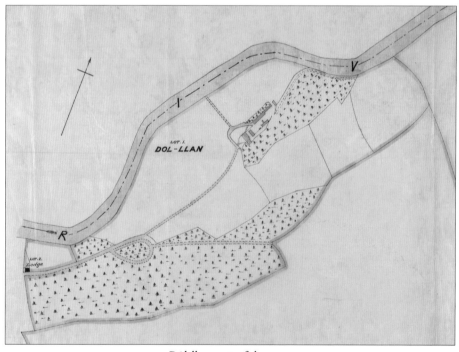

Dôl-llan map of demense.
(Photograph: Steve Dubé from sale particulars of *c*.1874).

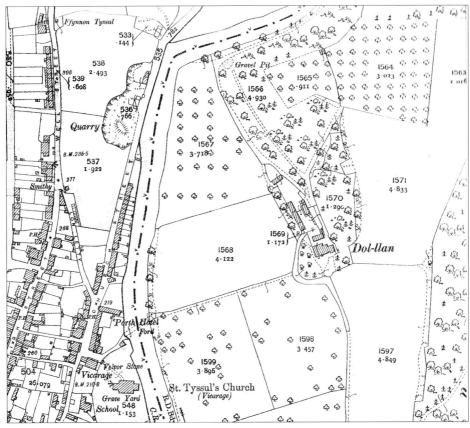

OS Map, 1905.

Cardiganshire homes.
(Illustration from *Gwilym Marles* by Owen M. Edwards, 1905).

Tyssul Castle – now known as Cae'r Bryn.
(Photograph: Steve Dubé).

Llandyssul from Dôl-llan (old postcard).

*Llandysul from church tower
(old postcard).*

*Llandysul from church tower
(old postcard).*

Bridge Street, Llandyssul (old postcard).

Pont Tyweli, Llandyssul (old postcard).

Penpwll, Llandyssul (old postcard).

Thurs 12th Alas as I was coming home by Dolgrogwys from Llanfair I took only one bottle of porter and then got Drunk.

The entries for next six days, from April 13 to 18 are limited to the single word, "Ill" – it appears that Rees was on an alcoholic binge.

Thurs 19th Dr Davis attended me twice today as I was much worse than had never [*sic*] been before.

Sat 21st Last night I enjoyed not a minute's sleep but all the time quite delirious talking to my departed brothers & positively thinking they or they [*sic*] messengers were in the room with me and could not keep myself in bed as the talk took all my attention. O what a time. Little did I think that I should get delirious by drinking. O Merciful Father take me now from this world if I shall ever drink again or even taste a drop.

Sun 22nd Betsy & Hannah my servants are acting as devilish against me as they possibly can. I have no other alternative but [to] dismiss them both & tomorrow I intend informing them so. I still feel very unwell & miserable in the extreme.

MAY 1860

Tues 1st At home all day, Br Evan came to my bedroom when I was in bed last night & began to talk me up about his account most terrible. I got so much frightened by his language & demeanour that I could not sleep all night. To the village/office about my mother's affairs. Drank six glasses of Beer & got very uncomfortable.

Thurs 3rd Very warm day. I am truly completely exhausted after been [*sic*] searching and examining my late brother's papers in order to find some documents relating to the lunatic at Pantyporthmon.[54]

Sat 5th At home all day, fine and warm; about setting mangles. My mind is most terrible indulging itself in the violation of the 12. No reading of R's[55] or prg[56] in the woods more than three times this year. Something most likely will soon happen to me.

Thurs 10th To Newcastle Emlyn fair to buy cows for Llanfair. Very rainy day. All kinds of fruit especially cherries are exquisite to be seen, all white with leaves not extended yet. There are more blossoms on this year than I ever remember before. Every thorn bush is with white garment. O what a beautiful sight to see the buds & blossoms of spring transmuted into flowers and foliage.

Sat 12th To Llanfair & then got drunk with porter.

---

54. Like Rees Thomas with his late brother's papers, I have been unable to trace this "lunatic".
55. Rules.
56. Praying?

The following five days are marked "intox" or are illegible until the entry for the 17th is simply: "Bewildered".

Sat 19th All apple trees are this week in full blossom & most delicious the fragrance they emit. Everything goes on well except Betsy & Hannah who are both lazy [and] negligent. The chickens and ducklings that have been hatched are all dead from neglect in giving them feed. They have carried bushels of corn to the fowls but afterwards neglecting to bring the eggs to the house, therefore if I say [a] word to one of them then I get such horrid & unwarrantable abusive language that all say now openly that I only keep Betsy as a wh—e.[57] I lost Dr Davis serv't Girl, otherwise would not be here today.

Sun 20th Jenkin was there for a very short time after we went into the house. He appeared to be indignant with me and as Evan Griffiths and myself were returning I swore on the New Testament in his presence as a witness that I would abstain from all intoxicating drinks from that day to the last day of the present year, and I hope to G-d[58] that I will observe this oath unviolated [*sic*], otherwise how can I show my face again.[59] Spent this Sunday again like every Sunday without cultivating in the least my moral faculties.

Thurs 24th [scrawled entry] Lire Com Lt Ls with the old My D ### ### [illegible] Dgr all int'ly. My moral character is at its lowest ebb, all in consequence of mon pg [illeg] in the woods. The sooner the better to change. Very hot day. Disgrace.[60]

Wednes 30th Idl Ls with m gbh good appedite [*sic*].[61]

The following day he resolves to begin "a new life once more", describing his "moral conduct" as "disgraceful".

JUNE 1860

[Written in top right hand corner of the page]: Set free from the 20th May by an oath before EGD.[62]

Mon 4th To Carmarthen after my affairs as an executor. Br Evan was there and sleeping on the settle at the Six bells[63] and was very pale in his countenance and apparently very much under the effects of drink. After coming home I was much offended at Betsy's conduct.

Wednes 6th The Union Benefit Club[64] procession.

---

57. The first suggestion of a sexual relationship with his servant Betsy.
58. Rees can never bring himself to write the word God in full.
59. The first of several pledges to give up drinking.
60. An entry replete with code that appears to relate to open-air sex with a neighbour, perhaps Mary Davies or David. The name reoccurs several times.
61. Once more Rees has sex with a neighbour.
62. His close friend Evan Griffiths, Dolgrogwys.
63. An inn located at what is now 7 St Peter Street, Carmarthen. The name refers to the six bells in St Peter's parish church. Two more were added in 1904.
64. Most of the public houses in Llandysul had their own welfare club. This was probably the one attached to the Union.

Thurs 7th Betsy is good for nothing. Her only work is doing so much injury to my moral character as possible.

Fri 15th Preparing the accounts as the Rev'd T. Evans comes here this afternoon. Down with him late at night. Serv't Betsy, as when strangers here, in a terrible temper and refuses to make dinner for him & myself, however is doing everything as I wish her today. O what a d—l[65] girl Betsy is.

Sat 16th Rev'd T. Evans & David Lewis here, the former preparing the accounts of the succession & personal duty accounts of my late brother T, the latter the accounts of my David & Evan. Serv't Betsy is in a terrible rage since yesterday. She today refused to bring dinner, tea and everything to us there, and further she tried to interrupt [?] Hannah to do the same. I told her to prepare herself for leaving on next Monday morning.

Sun 17th Chapel at am. Met the children of Llanfair, Anne & Mary, with Jenkin at Penpwll. Returned my thanks for coming here, that they may understand that I take it as a contempt on their part not coming near me & staying too at Tyssil castle for so many days. I can't much blame on them as Jenkin advises to be as contemptible to me as possible. Hearing Gwilym Marles pm.[66]

Mon 18th Betsy & Hannah absented themselves from home all yesterday. The former not doing any kind of work since Friday and further prevents her co-servant to do anything. Words can never express the temper that grieves Betsy for the last days. The sooner the better for me to let her go about her business and so I am determined to dismiss her this week. As soon as I came down this morning I was presented with a month's warning with Hannah written yesterday by "Montalembert".[67] I had no breakfast, both my servants refused to bring anything before. First swarm of bees rose at half past 2pm & they were irritable and [it] was dangerous to go near them. Informed the Rev'd T. Evans of the conduct of my servants and he advised me to dismiss both as soon as possible.

Tues 19th Rev'd T. Evans here at am, then left by coach to Carmarthen. The insane and desperate Betsy has not yet since Friday done anything in the way [of] work. Hannah is cooking my food and everything & greatly she proclaimed all about the house at the village & to everyone she meets, telling all kinds of lies. The talk about my servants & myself is indeed enough to drive me to do some bodily harm to them as really there never was any precedents to them.

Fri 29th Change of weather is likely. The two swarms are fed with honey but for the purpose as they have not yet had weather for honey gathering, consequently many swarms have already died in this neighbourhood. Nephew (David) here. Evan Thomas Nantegryd wrote (per Montalembert) to me requesting the accounts in order to have them examined & if approved that he would sign the Release.

---

65. Devil.
66. Gwilym Marles – the Rev'd William Thomas (1834–1879), Unitarian Minister, poet, editor and school teacher in Llandysul, great-uncle of Dylan Thomas.
67. This appears to be a nickname. Could it refer, ironically perhaps, to Charles Forbes Comte de Montalembert (1810–1870), a prominent and controversial London-born French politician and writer?

Sat 30th To Carmarthen respecting the accounts of Evan, the Rev'd T. Evans was at Aberayron. Had a long conversation with Messrs Morris & Thomas respecting the accounts. Dry, cold day. Arriving home about 6, then went to Llanfair. Too much work & trouble by ½ of late. My mind is constantly indulging itself in the abuse of the 12.[68]

JULY 1860

Mon 2nd Most part of the day at home preparing Br Evan's accounts, who threatens me with law suit & giving all kinds of abuse.

Tues 3rd David and Jonny were very indignant for desiring them to prepare a lesson every day. Jenkin came here last night and showed me a prospectus of a school sent him from Mr Jones Llwyn-groes. His manners were haughty and every word devolving supposed indignation to me. O what trouble I take about the affairs of the children of Llanfair.

Thurs 5th Making hay at Llanfair all day. Anne, Mary & David are dreadful to me, the latter only for the cause of my making him learn or prepare a lesson every morning, but he persists in refusing to learn anything. I am determined at all hazards to resign my executor and trustee ship after I pay the debts contracted to liquidate Llanfair's affairs.

Sat 7th Having the clover in at Llanfair & it was in pretty good condition. Mother took me up heartily for neglecting to weed about her house, but that was a shift cause for something else. No dinner or tea today.[69]

Mon 9th To the funeral of the late Mr Griffiths Horeb, returned from Horeb. It was not known whether my late brother John's funeral or that of today was the largest. My friend the Rev'd David Griffith Tavistock[70] arrived here today and has promised to stay for three weeks. Mother is here airing her house and the furniture therein. Betsy is to leave in a few days in consequence of her dreadful temper continually & Hannah is to leave this day week. Both will not do a thing that I ask of them.

Tues 10th Mowing finished. Servant Betsy, as when strangers here, is in a dreadful temper. Stated to her in a peacable [*sic*] way that I would lend her a cart to go away tomorrow morning and that it would be terrific if she was to abuse x*** the Servant of Llanfair when at dinner & in the presence & hearing of all here but was as usual useless to advise her.[71]

Wednes 11th Making hay all day. Rev'd David Griffith had the loan of Mercilass[72] again today. Betsy & Hannah understand that they are soon to leave my Service & so they are both as devilish

---

68. The diarist's 12 "rules".
69. The servants Betsy and Hannah still appear to be on strike.
70. Rev'd David Griffith (1823–1878), a native of Llandysul.
71. The diarist is presumably using the word "terrific" instead of "terrible".
72. A horse.

as possibly can be especially the former, who is really astonishing in her too readiness to abuse everyone. It is a sad thing to think that a woman is capable of such vileness.

Thurs 12th Sent a present of cherries to my respected Pastor. They were not very ripe. Also a small basket to Mrs James Wilks Head.[73] There is a picnic party on the top of Coedfoel. I was not invited as it seems that Jones the solicitor was the chief commander and provider for the occasion. The day is very hazy and nothing can be seen at any distance. I am very active about the hay harvest.

Fri 13th Having the hay in, about double the number of people necessary for the purpose but if one's service was refused it would cause a very great disapprovement. It rained a little before the last four loads we secured yet it was all put in the rick. In an addition to the trouble with about fifty hay maker, Dr Lloyd,[74] his wife and children, sister and her children, Miss Davis Llwyngroes and the children of Llanfair & Jenkin were here & all took Tea, & also Mrs Hall from Tenby. Such a lot never happened to be here before & really I was happy that my friend Mr Griffiths was at home as I could not possibly be with them all the time owing to the hay. Neither one of the children of Llangunllo[75] or Llanfair complied with my sincere request of staying here over the night. I felt that all consider me a person fit only to work & run for them as I am today, with the utmost contempt by all of them, and who at present is their best benefactor & has saved their property from being ruined by the run[?] of their late father's creditor. There is a large party at Tyssil Castle this afternoon. Mr Griffith was invited to dinner but I as an outcast of course, not invited.

Sat 14th To Llanfair at am. With Wynllan[76] trying for a salmon at Llyn Shorse at pm, not succeeding, though one was seen by Wynllan. I am going to try him after supper again. Very nearly com Idt Ls My but thank Gd kept away & now I am glad of it.

Wednes 18th The following names were the ladies & Gentlemen that were at Tyssil Castle last Tuesday. Three Misses Lloyds of Gilfachwen,[77] Dr Lloyd Carmarthen wife & family, Rev'd David Griffith Tavistock, Dr Davies & wife, Llangunllonians & the Llanverians.

Sat 21st To Carmarthen. Awful rain and thunder. Came without drinking anything all day but three glasses of cider. Unbearable Itg so com.[78]

Sun 22th [sic] To Llanfair at am. Chapel at pm. The Rev'd Dd Griffith preached there. He left here yesterday afternoon & is not returning before next Thursday. Betsy & Hannah are continually as negligent & obstinate to me as possible. They think that I can't have any after them.

---

73. Hanna James, wife of innkeeper and farmer John James at the inn on the Llanfihangel ar Arth side of Llandysul bridge.
74. Dr David Lloyd (1805–1863), Principal of the Presbyterian College, Carmarthen. His wife was Ellen (née Smith) of Swainby, Yorkshire, whom he married in 1853. They had two children, David Lewis and Lucy Ellen. [George Eyre Evans, *Lloyd Letters*, privately printed, 1908.]
75. The Davies family of Llangunllo. Dr Thomas Howell Davies, Rector of Llangynllo, married Rees's sister. Their children included David, Johnny, Grace, Mary Jane, Susannah Gwenllian and Frances Louisa.
76. Wynllan: James Rees, 62, parish clerk.
77. Daughters of the Rev'd Thomas Lloyd of Gilfachwen Isaf, Llandysul – Mary, Jane and Anna.
78. Another of the dairy's mysterious codes rendered as near as possible in conventional script. The phrase is often completed with the added form 'om' or 'on'. It possibly signifies sexual tension relieved by masturbation.

Wednes 25th To Llanfair am. Dr Lloyd & family there at pm.

Thurs 26th To Llanfair most part of the day. Dr Lloyd & wife have left Llandyssil this morning for home. They were both much displeased with me for not meeting there at Llanfair yesterday as they expected. Br Evan has another attack of Delirium tremens bad today. He is much better & is not in a dangerous state.

Fri 27th Rev'd D'd Griffith bade farewell to his friends & relatives today & he is leaving here tomorrow for Carmarthen. Br Evan has got over his attack of Delirium tremens again & he was down at Llandyssil yesterday walking all the way. Received the Draft of Release from Messrs M & Thomas. It is to be presented to Evan to be signed by him. Richard Jones curate Vaedrefawr here all the pm.

Sat 28th Rev'd Mr David Griffith left here for Tavistock this morning and I feel sorry after his good and agreeable company & much loss in truth it will be, especially to my morals. Mr Griffith carried on his love affairs with his intended (Miss Tilliter) by writing, either of them every day. To Llandyssil at pm to Mr Amphlett's,[79] then to the office (Jones) & when there David Evan[80] union came in & began to talk to me in a friendly way and really I did not understand at first that he was drunk. But after he came in the second time he was very much gone & now began to pick quarrels with me. However Jones prevailed upon him to go out, & apologised [to] me for his intrusion. Paid the Druggist for Br David the sum of £15.

Sun 29th Long before dawn from bed. At home all the pm excepting going to Llanfair. To Court Farm with David my nephew. The old Gentleman[81] was very kind to me yet he sometimes kicks me in the back. Begging of him to assist me to pay half of the money that I am obliged to pay for house at Dolmaen[82] but he peremtorily [sic] refused. Very late before arrived home.

Mon 30th To Llanfair this am. Anne & Grace Llangunllo[83] accompanied me by here to Tyssil Castle. **Com Ids Ls with my pretty girls – Shameful.[84]

AUGUST 1860

Wednes 1st To Llanfair. Anne & Mary left for school, the former for Chester, the other for Haverfordwest. Beginning cutting hay tomorrow under the farm yard of Llanfair.

---

79. Mr Amphlett's: James Amphlett, 35, of Black Lion, Llandysul. A frequently mentioned companion.
80. David Evans, 39, schoolmaster, son of John Evans, Union Tavern, innkeeper. [*Census, 1861.*]
81. John Evans of Court Farm, Cwrtnewydd.
82. Dolmaen: This farm of 146 acres is occupied in 1861 by 46-year-old John Lloyd and his wife, with six servants. [*1861 Census, Llanfihangel ar Arth.*]
83. Daughters of Dr Thomas Davies, Rector of Llangynllo, and his wife Margaret, Rees's sister.
84. That code again – perhaps this time for lascivious thoughts.

Thurs 2nd To Llanfair several times in the course of the day. David is too stupid to make himself ready to go tomorrow. John Thomas Shopnewydd[85] wrote at the request of Shony Domos[86] a very threatening letter that unless I would settle with him for Br David before 6 o'clock in the evening, proceedings would be taken against me. It was 6.15pm before the bearer handed the letter to me, so told her (bearer) to tell Shony to take his course and that I was quite ready for him.

Fri 3rd Much harassed by David [crossed through] messenger from Shony Domos & Evan Carp't Charlestown, both using threatening language, especially Shony Domos, who has already begun proceedings

Sat 4th To Llanfair early this morning. David returned to school. To Abercerdin to meet Jones solicitor relative to Shony Domos & Mother's affairs.

Sun 5th To Llanfair this morning. My niece Grace Llangunllo left here for home today. Gave her as pocket money ten shillings. Betsy accompanied her down.

Mon 6th At home all day. Jones Abercerdyn here trying to settle with me for Shony Domos.

Wednes 8th Took little Jonny of Llanfair to school to the Rev'd T. Thomas Cribor.[87] Poor fellow he was very sorry after home. Jenkin has returned from taking Anne to school. Br Evan is continually borrowing money of Jones solicitor in small forms and paying interest every fortnight for not paying it but it is to be added to the principal every fortnight & the amount he pays of interest at 7½ per cent.

Fri 10th To Llanfair remaking some of the hay Cocks but before 10am the rain began falling in torrents, so it continued all day. Betsy is endeavouring by every possible means to prevent doing anything for Llanfair. She is since yesterday unconscious of everything owing to her bad temper. I have no money to pay & dismiss her. Br Evan at Llanfair & was very angry with me yet he was speaking kindly in my face. Anne his servant left there yesterday, quarrelling with Evan & she was beaten with him very bad.

Mon 13th At Ffair Awst[88] with the fat cows of Llanfair. Conducted myself with the utmost propriety.

Wednes 15th My mind wandering in the abuse of the 12. Com Idt Ls with My Pen. [89]

Thurs 16th Betsy abuses me again today most terrible. It is really disgraceful for me to suffer such words from any one as from a servant girl. I have offered her wages but she refuses to take them so I am afraid that I must have recourse to physical force before I shall be able to drive her away.

---

85. John David Thomas, 39, draper, grocer and ironmonger of "New Shop". [*Census, 1861*.]
86. One John Thomas.
87. Rev'd Thomas Thomas. Ran a school at Pontsian.
88. *Ffair Awst* – an August fair.
89. Once again the code that the diarist uses to denote sex. This could be Mary Rees, a 24-year-old unmarried woman who lived with her brother at Penralltgerdin, next door to Dôl-llan.

Fri 17th To Llanfair Budding plums & cherries here. Rainy all day. Jenkin here at pm. He was in despondency & inclined to drinking. His servant girls gave him much trouble & inconvenience. Both of them are wild for boys.

Sat 18th The River is over flowing its banks larger than it has been for two years, but budding. James to Carmarthen with the butter of Llanfair. Terrible rainy day.

Sat 25th To Jones's office relative to mother's defaulters, which are to be proceeded with at the next County Court. Br Evan is once more poor fellow labour under Delirum Tremens. Neither Mother nor myself dares to go to see him as he is very angry with both of us.

Sun 26th Br David is daily affected with delusion, especially about Iolo Morganwg.[90]

Mon 27th Report of the cannons was well heard here & at Llanwenog last Sunday from Milford saluting the Great Eastern.[91]

Wednes 29th At Llanfair about the hay all day. Mother went up Nantegryd at the urgent request of Br Evan. Anne the servant has left there last week and most likely for the last time. Yes, everything is in an awful & neglected state. Sold an old cheese to Jenkin weighing 29lbs.

SEPTEMBER 1860

Sat 1st Making & having the hay in at Llanfair. It was ten o'clock before we finished. I was informed that Br Evan has gone down to Milford to see the Great Eastern accompanied with Dr Davis.

Tues 4th At Llanfair all day with the reapers. Br Evan came there and it seems that he was in much need of a sum of twenty pounds & most likely I would have lent him if I could.

Fri 7th Jim Bety, Shone Richards & Gwylim, son of the late Jacky Cilgwyn, had been here last night courting but neither Rachel nor Hannah went to them. They stole apples and pears & broke many of the branches of fruit trees and after I saw them, [I] went over to the police and brought him over with me to see the damage done to the trees and desired him to procure two summons to bring the Rascals before the magistrates at the next Petty Sessions. ** Com Idt with my p g b n **.[92] At Llanfair all the pm. Sister was there. Mother is indignant with me at present.

Sun 9th Long in bed. No chapel nor neither reading anything. To Llanfair with David Carp't Ffynnonbwla[93] & Evan Griffiths at pm. "—" Idling.

---

90. Iolo Morganwg is the bardic name of Edward Williams (1747–1826) the influential antiquarian, poet, collector, literary forger and creator of the *Gorsedd y Beirdd*, the picturesque cultural academy governing the ceremonies of the National Eisteddfod of Wales.
91. The *Great Eastern* – Isambard Kingdom Brunel's revolutionary steamship.
92. Another liaison with Mary Rees of Penralltgerdin?
93. David Titus, a 40-year-old carpenter living at nearby Ffynnonbwla.

Mon 10th To Llanfair & there most part of the day. Gwilim & Jim the fruit stealers came here this morning to ask my pardon for cutting and bruising the pear trees. Told them plainly & bluntly that I would not make up on any conditions with them & that I was determined to take them to the Petty Sessions. They were preceded by Thomas Cilgwyn bach who they thought [to] have some influence over me, but they were disappointed. Betsy's conduct is continually intolerable and I long to see Hollandtide[94] to get rid of her.

Tues 11th To Llanfair binding corn & getting the last hay in, also the second crop of clover. Hard hoar frost last night, consequently it has set a stop to all vegetable growth this season. Fine & warm, dry.

Thurs 13th Idt Ls with My P g b n.

Sat 15th To Llanfair this morning, remaining there all day. Very Stormy all the am. To the Wilks head[95] with few pears & plums at dusk. Also to Tyssil Castle. Just a few pears and plums to Miss Evans Pistill[96] & to Gwilym Marles & to Shop y Jones, but only a few to each place.

Sun 16th Heard a report that the Rev'd Evan Evans Llaethlliw had quarrelled with his wife & had kicked her as to cause a rupture. She is now at Llandrindod Wells. Montalembert is since tomorrow week to London accompanied with his brother Thomas & probably looking out for a situation [for] himself, also to his brother (T).

Wednes 19th To Llanfair early this morning, then to the fair,[97] where I conducted myself with the utmost propriety all day. No drinking, but certainly tasted a small [–] now and then from the hands of persons. Sold three oxen from Llanfair at £12 each, more of a £1 than other oxen of their age realised. To Llanfair after coming home from the fair. Mr Rees Thomas Cribor waited me back with the notice of paying David Blinebwey's aunt £1,000 up next Monday.

Fri 21st To Mr Price Glangwily[98] laying information against Jim & Gwilym for damaging a certain pear tree in the night of the 6th Inst.

Sat 22nd To Carmarthen. Very rainy morning. With my cart to fetch Beer for the sale at Llanfair.

Sun 23rd Chapel at am. Idling with Evan Griffiths at pm. No reading. The two Boys were served with summons yesterday by the policeman at Pencader.

---

94. Hollandtide – 12 November, the general day for letting lands, payment of rent, and for farm workers and domestic servants to take up their places for the year.
95. Inn on the Carmarthenshire side of Llandysul bridge.
96. Miss Evans Pistill, a neighbour.
97. *Ffair Medi* or *Ffair Mihangel* – September or St Michael's Fair.
98. John Lloyd Price, Glangwili (1803–1865), a magistrate.

Mon 24th To the Petty Session at Llanfihangel[99] with Jim & Gwylim for damaging the pear. The magistrates present were Mr Pryce, Capt Lewis,[100] Capt Elliott[101] & Mr Lloyd[102] Gilfachwen. The amount they had to pay was as follows. Fine £1 each. Damage 4/- ditto, costs 6/6d, in all £1.10.6 each, which they paid there. They never thought that it would be so much. This was the first case I have ever had to go to the Petty Session and am not sorry for it.

Wednes 26th At Llanfair early this morning. Began soon to bind corn. We were only 14 persons yet we bound and made into mow 78 mows. Very fine day, wind south East.

Thurs 27th At home all day with Evan Griffiths shooting. Shooting three rabbits, one pheasant & a partridge & gave them all to him.

Sat 29th At Llanfair. Finished binding corn there today. At my own corn here at pm. I wish to the sales at Llanfair to be over as all my time is taken up with the affairs there since my brother's death. I have the consolation to say that I have done my bit for the children.

Sun 30th With Evan Griffiths Dolgrogwys to Llwynrhydowen at am. To Pantydefaid Chapel at pm. Gwilym Marles preached in the former & one Rev'd John Davies Dancoed[103] in the latter. Both delivered excellent sermons. So ended September 1860.

OCTOBER 1860

Mon 1st To Llanfair all the am. Out with the people binding here at pm. Many salmon were captured about her last week by worm, fly & net. Betsy is terribly ill tempered since yesterday. She is quite a plague to live with here.

Tues 2nd With E. Griffiths to Llanfair & afterwards went salmon fishing with Wynllan, but not successful. The Commissioners are holding a meeting relative to the salmon fishing in Wales. Many fishermen from Llandyssil have gone down to Newcastle Emlyn for the purpose of attending the said meeting.

Mon 8th To Llanfair sale when I conducted myself with the utmost propriety. There were very large attendance of people and the corn realised good prices. The day was beautifully fine & everything went off uncommonly well except the hay, for which there were no bidders & so remained unsold.[104]

Tues 9th To Llanfair early this morning again looking about the corn. Very windy.

---

99. Llanfihangel ar Arth, where the magistrates usually sat at the Eagle Inn opposite the parish church.
100. William Price Lewes of Llysnewydd (1813–1890).
101. Thomas Elliott, Dolhaidd (*c*.1824–1870).
102. Rev'd Thomas Lloyd, b.1803, Rector of Llanfair Orllwyn.
103. Rev'd John Davies (1836–1922), Unitarian Minister, born at Tancoed, Llanwenog.
104. The sale of effects at Llanfair following the death of the diarist's brother. Preparing everything for the occasion had created a lot of work and scant reward for the diarist.

Wednes 10th To Llanfihangel fair. Terrible rainy day. Got Hf drunk.

Thurs 11th To Llanfair early this morning. Not well from the effects of yesterday.

Fri 12th Sent a reply to Mr John Lloyd Gilfachwen[105] to permit him to shoot over some farms of my late brother's. I am desired by Jenkin to go down to Tyssil Castle every day to look over his affairs during his absence with the militia and as I promised I go down every day and I go twice to Llanfair every day.

Mon 15th To Llanfair at am. To Tyssil Castle at pm. Hired Anne Llanfair[106] for the ensuing year for £8.

Thurs 18th Llanfair all the am. To Mr Jones office at pm. Br Evan is squandering money most awfully at present & is coming down every night to the village and borrowing money every week of Jones, paying 7½%.

Mon 22nd At Llanfair all day preparing thing for the sale.

Tues 23rd At Llanfair all day. Very busy and now much exhausted.

Wednes 24th Llanfair sale; very favourable day, though rather rainy especially late in the evening. Finished selling about half past 6.[107]

The diarist spend most of the next four days at Llanfair sorting things out and trying – but failing because of the weather – to complete the corn harvest.

Tues 30th Br Jenkin arrived from Aberystwyth last night. Received a form of notice from the Rev'd T. Evans to the effect of having the mortgages of Br Evan up to be paid to him in hard cash as he still refuses to sign the accounts for release the draft. He is entirely governed by Montalembert, who is there every day.

Wednes 31st To the new fair[108] at Llandyssil & there got drunk and even more foolish than I ever had been before. "—"

NOVEMBER 1860

There follows six days where the diary reads only DK for drunk or "bewildered", followed by the usual deep regret.

Wednes 7th Dreadful mental anguish. No sleep last night. Went late in the evening over to Jones's office relative to Mother's and Br Evan's affairs. Very nervous & debilitated & very profuse perspiration, frightening at the presence of children. O what misery I have once more brought on myself.

---

105. A law student, and son of the Rev'd Thomas Lloyd, Rector of Llanfair Orllwyn.
106. Anne Thomas, aged about 24, housemaid.
107. The second of two sale days at Llanfair.
108. *Ffair Gytuno.*

Thurs 8th Heard a lecture last evening by the Rev'd James Kilsby Jones[109] on self built men & really was very interesting. Today went shooting. Thank God I feel myself recovering once more.

Fri 9th Sister here at pm. Today sent David Davis Serv't Llanfair with notice to Velincwm requesting that widow to pay me on the mortgage. Betsy uses her abusive language towards me most liberal. What an awful fool I shall be if ever I shall have to suffer so much with anyone as I do almost every day with Betsy. The fact is that I would ten times rather begging my bread then to live with her.

Sat 10th Dio Pencnwc & his wife came to live to Llanfair today.[110] Poor mother was looking very sad all day. Stayed there most part of the day myself, though I feel very unwell myself. Not had a minutes sleep all last night from great pain in my chest. Dio Fynnonbwla[111] was served with a notice to quit from E. Griffiths today, Betsy in a desperate rage all day.

Mon 12th To the Druggist shop & then, owing not being well, drank a few glasses of brandy & got DK.

Tues 13th Unwell as usual from the damnable effects of alcohol. Rainy day. Low spirited, partly in consequence of the servants preparing to leave.

Wednes 14th James & Hannah left their service this afternoon. Betsy (if not rainy) intends leaving at 12 tonight. Mother came over from Llanfair but not to stay.

Fri 16th Betsy left tonight in our cart. I got DK.

Sat 17th Int all day. Betsy returned owing not being there in time for the 6 o'clock train.

Again it's all too much for our diarist who goes on another drunken binge until . . .

Tues 20th Bewildered and very ill too [*sic*] effects of DK.

Wednes 21st To Llanfair today. Awfully rain, the Tivy overflowing its banks. Very unwell still from the effects of the last debauch. Began once to pray & read my rules.

Thurs 22nd Betsy left at 12 o'clock last night in our cart for Carmarthen in order to be ready to start this morning by the six o'clock train. She left once before last Friday but was not there in time for the train and she returned again in my cart on Saturday & then remained here again all last night & her luggage was left at the station. She was perfect, honest, upright and straightforward in all her transactions. The only fact I had against her was her temper. Her wages were £12 & I gave her again on leaving £1.1.6d gift and on the whole she deserved that amount. She was found always

---

109. James Rhys Kilsby Jones (1813–1889).
110. New tenants at Llanfair.
111. David Titus the carpenter.

at home, Sundays included, so I must feel rather sorry after her and she too was very reluctant to leave. But I had no alternative but [to] dismiss as long as she refused to live with Br David here & that was the sole cause of my dismissing her. I wish her prosperity & happiness as long as she lives.[112]

Br Evan was served with a writ today by Jones Llandyssil at the Druggist there to recover £81 for drink. Mother consequently vexes very much. I sent to him to meet me at Llanfair tomorrow morning and if [he] will there sign the accounts & the Draft of the Release I will find him the money. Probably he will as usual refuse to come to any terms with me & the writ will take its course.

Fri 23rd To Llanfair all day. Br Evan came there & he refused to sign the accounts or the Draft of the Release. He was [a] good deal under the effects of drink & every symptom of an early grave in his countenance. He is an object to be pitied. Fine warm day, the birds sang this morning just as if it was an April morning.

Sat 24th From home all day so thank Gd I am once more restored to my senses & begin to enjoy the fine feelings of nature.

Sun 25th This day for the last time I swore on the New Testament & before David Davis, Br of Mally Farm that I should abstain entirely from tasting a drop of any intoxicating beverages from today to the 31st of December 1861. The oath is written on a paper to be read every morning. It took in the little house at Pencastle Garden at 4pm as I [was] just returning from chapel. May the Almighty God assist me to observe it.

Mon 26th Mother, Br David & little Jane left Llanfair to come to live here today. It was a very cold day, high wind blowing from the East. Mother and Jane went to live in their own house & David here with me.[113]

Tues 27th To the meet of Gogerddan Fox Hounds at Bwlchbychan. Found a fox on the bank of Dolwallter, followed him pretty fast to Llanwen Llanfair and from there to Bank Sychty, where he was given up.

Thurs 29th At home all the am. To Llanfair at pm. Br Evan here also at am. He is for the last nine days sleeping almost all his time & drinking as hard as ever. He still resists signing the accounts notwithstanding the writs which has [*sic*] been served upon him. By his present appearance he cannot live but a very short time.

DECEMBER 1860

Mon 3rd [crossed out] (The boys here to courting Anne. She is wild for going to them.)

---

112. There is little doubt that Betsy was at the very least an occasional lover for the diarist, who here reveals some of his feelings for her, contrasting his earlier observations – see March 14 and June 15, 16 and 19 in particular.
113. "their own house" is an adjoining dwelling attached to the mansion.

Tues 4th Betsy sent for another character [reference] to me. Wrote in for her to a Batchelor. Br David is very useless & very loquacious all day. There is no sense coming out but almost about Iolo's & such like.[114]

Wednes 5th Pantydefaid timber sale. Serv't Anne informed me this evening that she was engaged to Shame[115] the son of Ianto mason & that her lover was here last night & that he was coming again tonight, and so he came. I am much disappointed with Anne for coming here at all well knowing that she is privately engaged & talks about getting married soon. No good will come of her here and the sooner for me to have one instead of her the better.

Thurs 6th In great trouble of mind for being so much disappointed with Anne. I now begin to detest her for showing so much duplicity and she tries to go over me by her cunning & she has succeeded to a large degree as I have been very liberal to her, but I shall mark her henceforth.

Sat 8th Anne is [the] most cunning girl that I ever had yet. She pretends that she cares but little about Shames and practices all kind of duplicity towards me. I am very sorry that I ever hired such a creature at all. However I intend to be up with her in every way.

Sun 9th To Llwynrhydowen Chapel to hear Mr Fitzwilliams[116] preach an English sermon. His sermon was short & the Rev'd William Thomas the Minister[117] delivered in Welsh, verbatim et literatum. His text was on St John, 10 ch 9 verse.[118]

Tues 11th To Llanfair at am. Attempted to ** com Idt Ls with R – l D – d[119] but thank Gd failed.

Wednes 12th To Carmarthen. Very late when coming home & very cold. Had not tasted a drop all day. Servant Anne has promised never to go to her lover any more. Time will prove the truth.

Thurs 13th To Llanfair. S't Anne has today again promised never to go to her present lover any more. I am afraid that she is a girl of very great duplicity & does not care what to say to me.

Fri 14th Mr O. Jones Penrallt, his father, uncle, John James Penbont & myself were shooting over this land today. Shot six woodcocks, four pheasants & three rabbits. We startled two hares by Dolgrogwys & saw about a dozen woodcocks.

---

114. Diarist's younger brother David, a problem for the family because of his unpredictable behaviour. David is obsessed with Iolo Morganwg, the bardic name of Edward Williams (1747–1826), the influential Welsh antiquarian, poet, collector, and literary forger who established the Gorsedd y Beirdd or Order of Bards that still provides the pageantry of the National Eisteddfod.
115. Shames = James.
116. Edward Crompton Lloyd Fitzwilliams (1807–1880), radically-minded lawyer and squire of the Cilgwyn estate, Llandyfriog.
117. Gwilym Marles.
118. St John, Ch. 10, verse 9: "Some said, This is he: others said, He is like him: but he said, I am he" – a blind man cured by Jesus.
119. Rachel David?

Sat 15th [scrawled] Servant Ann with me in bed all night **nearly cum Ilt Ls however not succeeded. Dge etly.[120] Too drowsy, no chapel nor neither any religious reading, but horrid remorse for my disgraceful conduct, which will soon bring ruin and unbearable shame on my head.

Mon 17th To Llanfair. Out shooting in Dolgrogwys at pm. I have given myself up for the last fortnight to passions in common with the brute and am to [sic] disgraceful to think of reading my Rules or anything else good.

Wednes 19th Br Evan signs the Draft of Release today, and the longstanding accounts which he refused to do now for nine long months. My plan by stopping him to have any money brought him soon to settle. Sent him on two notes of hand, the sum of £200, which I shall borrow from the bank next Saturday. Snow 5 inches over the ground.

Thurs 20th Second timber sale at Llanfair. The earth covered with snow to the depth of 4½ inches. Suffered more cold in my legs today than ever before. Hard frost.

Fri 21st To Penpompren Llanwenog meeting Mr Roberts solicitor, Mr Evans road sweeper Llan-rhystud & Mr Evans Court relative to the affairs of Llaethliw.

Sat 22nd Terribly cold morning. Very hard frost & the earth white with snow. Paid bills for Br Evan & for whose affairs I was obliged to go to town this awful day. Been to the Rev'd John Evans,[121] Jones & Barker solicitors,[122] Messrs Morris & Thomas, to Wilkins Bank,[123] Mr T. Williams. Very late before I left town & most happy owing that I had not tasted a drop of any intoxicating beverages all day.

Sun 23rd The earth covered with snow still, accompanied with frost & very cold, but better at pm when it began snowing again.

Tues 25th Xmas day, to the village. Seeing little fireworks at night. Very cold. Apples & mangles all frozen. The river frozen over in many places.

Wednes 26th To the office (Jones) relative to Mother's affairs. Dk Ginger resin wine at the Druggist & Tyssil Castle till quite drunk and consequently made a complete fool of myself. Very cold & high wind & snow drifts were formed.

Fri 28th At Nantegryd with the Release to be signed by brother Evan, which he did, & witness by Rees Thomas Cribor fawr, so everything is finished with my executorship with Evan. Br Evan here at night very angry.

---

120. Dge etly: discharge externally; the diarist notes on such occasions whether or not he was able to practise coitus interruptus.
121. Believed to be the Rev'd John Evans (1835–1888) who was at that time in Carmarthen College.
122. John Hoyes Barker, Carmarthen-based solicitor.
123. Wilkins & Company had branches in Brecon, Merthyr Tydfil, Carmarthen, Haverfordwest, Cardigan, Llanelly, Aberdare and Cardiff. [*Carmarthen Antiquary*, Vol. IV, Parts 3 & 4, 1963.]

Sat 29th Ferreting rabbits at Gallt Pen allt gerdyn with E. Griffiths, John Rees David Yetwen.[124] Captured six. Awfully cold & windy day, that snow drifts are forming this evening.

Sun 30th Thawing. Not much snow is visible this evening, except when snow drifts existed. Chapel at am.

Mon 31st Rainy & stormy at night. Thomas Rees Tailor,[125] and a worthy friend of mine, expired between 4 & 5 o'clock yesterday morning of Hydrothorax. He had been very delicate for many years & had he not a perfick [sic] knowledge of his disease & its treatment he would have been in his grave many years ago. He was a quiet & inoffensive man & every [minute?] he had to spare was given to reading. His funeral is tomorrow. This year is about to expire & by reflecting on my life during the past year I find that it has [been] spent not merely to no avail to myself but highly immoral, & I am afraid that I am in my morals at present much lower than I was this day last year. However it is not yet too late to improve & to make a better use of my time in future.

1861 JANUARY

Tues 1st Funeral of Twmi Daniel[126] Into.[127]

The funeral signals the start of another binge. Dr Davies calls on the fourth day (Sat 5 January). It appears to cost Rees Thomas about £5 in "Spt" – either the amount of alcohol consumed in this time or the bill from Dr Davies. The following day is recorded as "half dead getting sober" and the entry for Monday 7 January has the single word "bewildered" that often signalled the end of the binge.

Tues 8th To Carmarthen awfully low Spt & terribly cold day. The earth is still covered with snow. Jenkin is daily coming here & daily incites Mother to be (if possible) more angry with me for my conduct last week.

Wednes 9th To Llanfair at am. Thawing. Br Jenkin is still very busy in deteriorating my moral character. He took the two boys (nephews) from me after I got drunk. They are, as he styles himself, a happy family at Tyssil Castle. O Lord let me not run into extremity. Mother prevents little Jane from entering this house since I fell last week. O what a being I am represented by my relations. Never can I come so intimate with any of them as before and never shall I wish too [sic]. I am somehow or other in most desponding this evening, but certainly I am not to be pitied, nor neither to be trodden down so much under my relatives foot as I am at present.

Thurs 10th Had to send twice & threatening to go myself to Tyssil Castle before Jenkin & Anne would permit Jonny to come here to go to school today and if they were at home when the last messenger was sent he would not be allowed then but they both had left for Carmarthen and little

---

124. David Davies, a 40-year-old widower and agricultural labourer with two children. [*1861 Census, Llandyssil.*]
125. Thomas Rees, son of Daniel Rees. Believed to have lived at Quarry, Llanfihangel ar Arth.
126. Thomas Rees.
127. Intoxicated again.

Jonny was released and went to school. Jenkin & Anne were much enraged & uttered the most abusive language against me to Watty. Awfully excited myself all day.

Fri 11th To Rhydfydwydd measuring the work of the carpts & masons there. Thawing, but very cold. Jenkin & the children went to Court Farm to make false complaints against me. Mother is dumb to me since last Monday week. Very unwell all day.

Sat 12th Old Xmas Day & very unhappy day upon me, very miserable to the extreme. At home & in the house all day. I now begin to find that Servant A is a most treacherous and cunning Girl. She takes much pains to remove every suspicion I have of her sincerity & truth. This day has proved what a thing she is.

Mr Evans has sent Anne his serv't to me with a writ of summons from the County Court to the suite of Ianto Bribwll[128] for £2.

Mon 14th To the office & Shop Penybont after dark. Settled with Jones the Shop re his bills against my two late brothers, also against David (brother) & my nephews & nieces very late in the evening. Jenkin is most busy fabricating lies against me, that is all his work at present.

Tues 15th Rent audit day of Llanfair. There all day. Jenkin & the children at Court Farm. Much exhausted.

Wednes 16th To Carmarthen. Very cold & frosty day. Taste some drink. To Jones office at night relative to Llanfair's affairs. Serv't A with me in b–d. Dge but all externally. Jenkin & the children all busy in fabricating lies upon me and M[other] is dumb to me.

Thurs 17th Arranging the accounts book. Very active but awfully low Spirited all day, repenting that I ever took the affairs of Llanfair upon me.

Fri 18th Marking Fir to be cut at Gallt Penalltgerdyn. Drunk an 1s worth of Br conjointly with EG & Jn Rees, then dreadfully low spirited. Anne's intended was here tonight, she did not go out but spoke to him for three hours in the window.

Sat 19th To Llandyssil after dusk paying my bill & other amounts borrowed of Mrs Jones Shop. Dreadfully low spirited ever since my last fit of intoxication the beginning of this year. God only know what will become of me if I will continue much longer in this miserable state of existence, no appetite, no sleep & no trust for anything, but hardly able to talk particularly loud. Servant Anne in bed *[written in a scrawl]*.

Sun 20th E. Griffiths here at am. Chapel at pm. Jenkin & the children at Chapel in their carriage. They all passed me without taking notice of me at all, especially David.

---

128. Probably Evan Rees, 70, carpenter. [*1861 Census, Llanfihangel ar Arth.*]

Tues 22nd To the office of Mr Jones Sol'r only for a chat. Also to Mr Evans Pistill Storehouse.[129] Servant A n e with me in bed tonight. Com Idt Ls with her and perhaps little Dcge <u>internally</u> not quite certain too, but took this as a most serious warning. Been to Court Farm today and also to Nantegryd. My morals are awfully low at present. Somehow or other I feel l o – e for S't A n e.[130]

Wednes 23rd Very low Spirited tonight in consequence of last night's affair. Very sleepy all day.

Thurs 24th At the office at am examining preparing books for medicine to be provided with at the next County Court. Was there for 3 hours.

Fri 25th At Mr Jones's office all am examining & arranging the medical books.

Sat 26th At Llanfair all day planning the new orchard. Late at Llandyssil last night. I have but very little pleasure to do hardly anything relative to Llanfair's affairs not partly owing to the children turning out to be such spendthrifts & stupid to me.

Sun 27th S't A n e last night with me in bed. <u>Com Idt dge no certainty</u> [*underlined in text*] whether all <u>extly</u> or not. The sooner the better for me to discontinue so doing. At home all day, drk a few glasses of brandy today & last night. Terrible mental anguish all day. In bed most part of the day.

Mon 28th To Llanfair at pm. To the office of Mr Jones for about 3 hours at night examining the bills of the defaulters of Mother. Alas S't a ne in b d to night again. Com Idt Ls with her not certain whether <u>all the Dge was extly</u> yet I think so every time yet.

Thurs 31st To Nantegryd at Br Evan's request relative to making a pnt [?] & planting Fir trees. He is unwell himself. To Jones's office relative to Mother's and Evan's affairs. There for about 2 hours. S't A ne in b d com Idt Ls with h r. <u>Dge all extlly.</u>

FEBRUARY 1861

Fri 1st Made a most solemn oath before E. Griffiths Dolgrogwys to the effect that I would abstain from all intoxicating drink from this day to the last day of the current year. This shall be my last oath. O may I observe it for my own sake.

Sun 3rd Lounging at am, Chapel at pm, but while there quite drowsy with wandering thoughts. Rather chilly, dry. Remonstrated with S't Anne for not coming home in time after been [*sic*] to her own home. She took it as a great insult and cried.

---

129. Mr Evans Pistill Storehouse: This is unlisted in the 1861 census, although Pistyll was a substantial building in Llandysul's main street.
130. This sentence is an exact reproduction of the diary and shows the diarist's tendency not to spell things out when they touch upon a raw feeling.

Mon 4th At Llanfair all day. Found out that S't A is full of roguery & duplicity and her policy is always to keep the truth from me as much as possible. I wish I never had hired her or that All Hallowtide[131] was near.

Tues 5th Alas Com Idt Ls with S't A late lt night. Dge <u>almost quite certain all extlly</u>.[132]

Thurs 7th To Mr J. Sol's office at dusk relative to Mother's affairs. There are with her at present in the County Courts above 20 persons. Had a very sharp discourse today with the person that keeps a public house of Rhyddlan. His bill for ale amounts to nearly £10. Br E here after supper for a long time. I avoided seeing him at all.

Fri 8th Very drowsy at am. Planting young fruit trees & gardening at pm. Very wet & rainy. Com Idt Ls with A. <u>Dge all extlly</u>. 1—2 Disgraceful.

Mon 11th Ffair Gwl fair day.[133] Frost last night. At home all day. Gwilym Marles here for two hours at night. Promised to fetch a load of coal for him from Carmarthen. Com Idt Ls with S't A but Dge <u>all extlly</u>. I am certain that I have not yet caused any unfavourable result.

Wednesday 13th S't A intended Jim here last night. I cannot know whether she has been out, but to a certainty I think she has.

Thurs 14th This day 12 month the corpse of my late brother Thomas was consigned to his Grave, my mind was dwelling on that mournful occasion all day till I became at night quite despondent.

Sat 16th Once more Com Idt Ls with S't A twice last night. Dge I <u>think all extlly</u>. I now plainly find & prove that I am fast running headlong into destruction. No reading of Rs or any this today in consequence of last night, never reading anything but all day conscious of the sure result of my conduct, which will soon put an end to my life. Very wet and rainy.

Mon 18th After the Gogerddan Fox hounds, startled a fox from Bwlchbychan plantations & lost him by Llanfair. Alas tonight again Com Idt Ls with S" A. <u>Dge all extlly</u>.

Tues 19th Preparing David's accounts with David Lewis all day. Very low spirited entirely in consequence of m-l c-duct.[134] Very rainy at am. I have not enjoyed any of the fine feelings of nature yet since B'y left,[135] but labouring under great mental trouble owing to what will surely fall upon me.

The next four days are almost entirely spent doing family accounts, helped by David Lewis.

---

131. Halloween – and a hiring fair.
132. Diarist is now sleeping with his servant Anne more and more.
133. *Ffair Gŵyl Faer* – the Mayor's Festival Fair.
134. Moral conduct.
135. Still lamenting Betsy's departure.

Sat 23rd Again Com Idt Ls with S't A this mng. Dge all extlly. I went to Carmarthen today relative to Llanfair & David's affairs. Over head & heels in trouble. Wilkins Bank refused to release the note for £200 so I must find them by next Wednesday without fail. O what trouble I have.

Mon 25th About 2 o'clock this morning Com Idt Ls twice with S't A. Dge all extlly. Found her today a complete liar & double faced. She has been twice, including today, at the Wesleyan Chapel meeting Jim, who is accompanying her part of the way home. They are sending letters to each other every week and I have reason to believe that he is coming here at night very often. She is the greatest rogue & liar that I ever found or heard. She tries by every possible means to deceive me in every way whatever. But she will not succeed as heretofor as I have already completely found her to be the most devilish dangerous creature that ever breathing & the sooner to dismiss her the better for me for me in one hundred respects. I have been so far exceedingly liberal to her but what a fool I have been or she has made of me. I would rather now than £20 if her year were up to dismiss her as I felt I cannot describe her great duplicity & cunning & will never in future believe a word what she says. I have found out more tricks of her than all the girls that have been here before put together. I look & speak kindly to her today. David Lewis here making the accounts.

Tues 26th About making up the accounts from morning to night. To Dolgrogwys for a walk at dusk. Mrs G was very cheerful & jocase [?] owing to her having secretly imbibed something of the nature of eau de vie. Beautiful day. Preparing myself at night to leave with cart for Carmarthen at 3 o'clock tomorrow morning.

Wednes 27th To Carmarthen for the purpose of going to London relative to Llaethlliw affairs but unfortunately receiving a letter stating that I was not necessary afterwards. Before leaving home this morning Com Idt Ls with S't A. Dge all <u>extlly</u>.

Thurs 28th Mr David Griffiths, a relative of the Rev'd John Thomas Black Lion, who is about leaving this world for his heavenly abode (he the said DG remains here still to see what will become of his uncle). This being the last day of this month, which I grieve to think how I have spent it, not merely wasting my time but for the many sins I have committed.

MARCH 1st 1861

Fri 1st To Llanfair & at pm to Mr Jones's office relative to the affair of building a new place of worship for Unitarians there. Promised to subscribe £12.12 towards the erection of the Chapel.

Sat 2nd Out ferreting rabbits all day. Very rainy & stormy at pm. Before rising this morning Com Idt Ls with S't A. <u>Dge all extlly.</u>

Tues 5th The Rev'd & respected Mr J. Thomas Blacklion died about 4 o'clock this morning. Sister came up today. David Lewis with me at the accounts all day. Not well myself.

David left here clandestinely for the village but fortunately stopped on his way to Tyssil Castle & came back with Sister, who happened to come here. He is very strong in body at present & will without the least provocation immediately threaten to strike me. However he has not yet carried his threat into execution.

Wednes 6th After the Gogerddan Fox hounds. Found two, not one killed. David left for Llandysul again today in a dreadful rage but he went to no house except Dio Cooper's & Tyssil Castle & afterwards returned with Jenkin. He is ready (as he often says) to kill me.

Fri 8th Making the accounts all day. David Lewis also here. Once more Com Idt Ls with S't A. Dge <u>all extlly</u>. Still there is danger owing to the cret-r-e[136] being full of cunning and treachery.

Sat 9th Funeral of the late Rev'd John Thomas. The Rev'd J. James preached at Pantydefaid on the occasion. His sermon was a very short one & was delivered with very great trouble owing to his giving way to ebutlition [*sic*] to feelings (crying).

Wednes 13th At home all day writing. Terribly low spirited. Br David in a continual rage, scolding most severely with dangerous threats upon everyone. It is really quite sufficient to cause anyone to go out of his senses by hearing him.

Thurs 14th David Lewis & myself making the accounts of Llanfair all day. Fine day but rain at night. Mother went in my cart to Carmarthen about 2 o'clock this morning to see somebody regarding her business. "Alas" Com Idt Ls with S't A but again this time <u>Dge all extlly</u>. That took place last night.

Sat 16th "Alas" Com Idt Ls with S't A twice. <u>Dge all extlly</u> almost to a certainty. Sent a horse to meet Mother at Llwyndafydd when returning from Carmarthen after last Thursday. Have spoken yesterday to Mr Pryse Bwlchbychan relative to removing the Post Office from Abercerdyn and he promised me to write to his brother the member to try not to have it removed as it is wish of the innocent Evanses.

Sun 17th Idling at am. To Dolgrowys at pm all evening chatting with E. Griffiths. This date three years ago Br John died. Read his funeral sermon today.

Sat 23rd Met Capt Sheraton[137] by Gorsgoch relative to Llanfair. Returned by Nantyrhyd & alas Got Dk there.

Sun 24th Int at Nantegryd all day. Shameful.

Mon 25th At home & there in bed all day. Com Idt Ls with S't A. Dge I think all extlly. Bewildered.

---

136. Creature.
137. Rees is evidently advertising Llanfair for rent. It is impossible to decipher the name of the prospective tenant from the diarist's handwriting. Capt Sheraton, or is it Thornton, Thordon or Thowton, for example, is interested. I have not been able to find any information about this person.

T-t-tler [teetotaller]

Wednes 27th Today began once more to read my Rules & pray from my heart in the wilderness for the first time this year. Felt much pleasure in fulfilling this duty.

Thurs 28th To the County Court at Newcastle Emlyn relative to Mother's & Llanfair's affairs.

Fri 29th Very unwell from Rheumatism. At home all day, to Llanfair at pm. Wrote to old S't By. I find a cause that admits a very great doubt as to the honesty of S't A during my last fit of Int. She is a person that takes a great advantage upon any being that makes himself helpless by drk.[138]

APRIL 1861

Tues 2nd Unwell & very low Spd, and "alas" Com Idt Ls with S't A. <u>Dge all extlly</u>. Miserable. Shame.

Wednes 3rd Met Capt Thordon at Llanfair. Failed to agree as to the rent of the house & ten acres of meadow. Offered the house, outhouses and the garden with ten acres of land for £75, but he refused to offer more than 60. Very unwell from a severe cold. Br Davies went as far as the Bribwll on his way to Carmarthen. Watty[139] went after him [and] brought him back. He is very savage & pugnacious these days.

Thurs 4th Br David is for the last three days much altered & worse in his senses, very restless, talkative, laughing and singing, more inclined giving way to bad temper. As he was going to Llandysul today my S't Evan & myself brought him back by force by Danrallt. He was kicking, striking and biting most terribly. Had Dio Farm[140] to follow & accompanying this afternoon. The children of Llangunllo here at pm. David is leaving for L'pool to be apprenticed as an ordinary seaman. Grace is returning to school to Bristol & Mary and Jane to Carmarthen. S't A has been out courting to Enoch mason[141] last Wednesday night. Confessed herself today. Take care, on my warning. To Jones office for no particular purpose.

Fri 5th To Aberayron to see the Rev'd Titus Evans, who is there for the benefit of his health since last Monday. He & Mrs Evans came down here & took Tea.

Sat 6th To Bwlchbychan relative to Llanfair at pm. Br David is getting more quiet & less threatening in his language now than he has been for the last four days. Rev'd T. Thomas Pantydefaid here at night. My cold is worse again. *** [smudged] with S't A for the last 3 days in consequence of having found her wild & double faced.

---

138. S't By = Servant Betsy. The diarist writes to the last servant he dismissed even as he suspects her replacement of turning, like Betsy, against him.
139. Walter James, 38, agricultural labourer living in Dolellan Lodge. [*1861 Census, Llanfihangel ar Arth.*]
140. Dio Farm = David Evans, Dolellan Uchaf, aged 67, farmer of 135 acres, one of the Dôl-llan tenants.
141. Possibly Enoch Jones of Blaenmain, Llanfihangel ar Arth, aged 22 in 1861, son of Elizabeth Jones aged 58, widow, hose knitter & pauper. [*1861 Census.*]

Sun 7th Rev'd T. Thomas left this morning. S't A was received as a member or communicant at Pantydefaid today. The cursed papers must be filed tomorrow. Fine but cold day.[142]

Tues 9th To Llanfair at am. In the garden at pm. Alas Com Idt Ls with S't A. Dge <u>all extlly</u>. I am fast running into destruction. Gd, what will become of me.

Wednes 10th To Llanfair to meet Capt Sheraton. Agreed with him about taking the place. Very fine & warm day & very lazy myself.

Fri 12th The Tivyside Fox hounds come hunting by here. Found a fox in Gwrtheyrn, lost him here again after running him by Penlan. Found another in Coedfoel, lost that one again. The day was dry, very warm. David is in better temper all day.

Mon 15th To Llanfair at am, out about selling potatoes at pm. Set the otter trap. Whitewashing the dwelling house. Anne & Mary write almost every week to Mother. They always assure to be kindly remembered to all their relatives except to me. I shall most certainly throw all their concern into Chancery very soon.[143]

Tues 16th Trapped an otter last night. Put him in the pond of the farm today. Many from Llandyssil came to see the dogs fighting with him. Our old Sam was by far the best dog.

Thurs 18th To Llanfair & Llandyssil, Ffair blodau fach. Conducted myself with the utmost propriety, being a Testator. To Mr Jones office relative to Tŷ hen. Capt Thowton began selling the Garden at Llanfair yesterday. I am too full employed these days, have too many irons in the fire.

Fri 19th To Llanfair at am & pm. Mother here at pm. Selling Dio potatoes. Very active all day. Very hot & dry. Br David locked S't Anne in the pantry of the Palan [?] all the am & she would be there still had not Mother heard her calling out. He purposely locked her up in order to try to find some Dk.

Sat 20th "Alas" Com Idt £Ls with S't A last night, however I am almost quite certain that <u>all Dge was extlly</u>, <u>too bad, too bad</u>. At Llandyssil all pm. Very hot day. Jenkin has not yet come home from taking David Llangunllo to Liverpool.

Mon 22nd The letting of the land sale at Llanfair. Let today £267.16.0 worth of land so had an excellent sale & was well attended with people.

Wednes 24th Poor sister it seems in consequence of Davis dissipated habits is in great pecuniary distress.[144]

---

142. The census was taken on the night of April 7/8.
143. The first mention of a long and complicated Chancery case involving a series of disputes over the will of Rees' dead brother Thomas Thomas (died 11 February 1860) which was eventually filed after Rees' death by Anne Thomas and her husband Evan Jones, 25 May 1868.
144. Rees' sister Margaret is evidently having problems with her husband Thomas Howell Davies, rector of Llangunllo.

Thurs 25th To Llandyssil all the pm. In very great uneasiness of mind owing that I am in awful danger of my creditors running upon me as I have borrowed very large amounts to liquidate the debts of Llanfair. Br Evan is squandering money like sand on the sea shore. An end to his extravagance must soon come.

Fri 26th To Llanfair. Out about selling mangles. Rain is much expected. Tivy very small & the soil quite parched up. Mother & myself counted the present debts of Br Evan up to £1,800. Plan must soon be formed to check his present extravagance, otherwise he will be in less than two years penniless.

Mon 29th Br Evan went himself on horseback as far as Alltwalis to meet his Serv't Anne[145] on her return from Carmarthen. He is giving away all his money to her. She says that he has made a will all in her favour & that I am afraid is true. Time will soon show.

Tues 30th To Llanfair & Tyssil Castle. Mother & two charwomen with my servants washing clothes under Penralltgerdin. Jones office at dusk. Com Idt Ls with S't A. <u>Dge all Extlly</u>. She tried for intly. Terrible attempt. Grand warning.

MAY 1861

Wednes 1st Fine warm day. No Bees this year, all dead. Out about selling mangles. The ground perfectly dry, grass very scarce here, sheep are suffering therefrom.

Thurs 2nd The Huntsman of Tivyside came with a letter from Mr Jones Penlan[146] asking for the exclusive right to hunting over my land and that of Llanfair. Stated that I should give him a reply in a few days. Very busy about Llanfair & Tyssil Castle all day. Finishing setting mangles. Weather hot & very dry. To Jones office at dusk relative to Evan's affairs. Mrs Davies Tŷ Hen[147] here today.

Fri 3rd Today I am 38 years of age. Mr Thomas Rhydowen[148] here. To Llanfair twice today.

Sat 4th To Carmarthen relative to my brother's affairs. I am at present in awful pecuniary difficulties. O what will become of me. I am in terrible mental trouble.

Sun 5th Loan to S't A today, 3/-. She went from Chapel home & promised to be back by 4 o'clock as Mr Evans Pistill was coming over, to accompany me to Llanfair after Tea. However A did not come home before dusk, this being the 6th time she went from home & only once she returned on time. Chapel at am.

Mon 6th To Llangunllo & alas there Gt DRK.

Another binge for the next two days.

---

145. Anne Oliver, aged 35, dairy maid. [*1861 Census.*]
146. David Jones, a farmer aged 45.
147. Unable to trace this individual.
148. David Thomas, aged 48, shopkeeper at Rhydowen.

Thurs 9th Hf Dk. Alas Com Idt with S't A & am not certain all Dge <u>extlly</u>. Disgraceful.

Fri 10th Terrible remorse. To Llanfair but very poorly all day. Shameful.

Sat 11th To Llanfair. Active, I find myself today once more, thank Gd, recovering. I once more find that there is no safety to me but in total abstinence, so I shall embrace it again in a few days.

Sun 12th Active reading at home all the am. Chapel at pm. Very miserable under the sermon owing that I was most terribly pierced by a guilty conscience. Heavy snow in the mountains this morning & very cold. Trees that had expanded there [*sic*] leaves are all burnt up by the frost on Wednesday & Thursday night last and all the potato leaves & young fruit.

Mon 13th Very active all, thank [God] I am once more in my usual strength & vigour again. In a day or two I intend making an oath before Evan Griffiths Dolgrogwys that I will have nothing to do with the damnable drink. Very fine & warm day.

Wednes 15th The mortgage of Velingwm paid up to Jones solicitor yesterday & he through Montalembert succeeded to get the foolish Evan to give him the control over the sum.

Thurs 16th Alas Com Idt Ls with S't A last night and <u>Dge</u> <u>little</u> internally. "<u>O what can I do, Gd</u> <u>knows</u>. Mother went to Nantegryd yesterday & today to prevail upon Evan to have his money from Jones solicitor as [soon as] possible but her begging is to no avail. He hastens to destruction by every possible means & so he will be penniless in less than two years.

Fri 17th Br Evan come here last night. Refused to lend any money to Mother or myself. He would have done so had he not been advised otherwise by Montalembert when coming over here. I told Evan plainly & bluntly in his face what sort of fellow he is & how he has treated me for the kindness showed him always. I got myself into bad temper and was so dreadfully excited as not to be able to sleep all night. Dk a strong glass of whisky & when that poison took effect Com Idt Ls again with S't A. <u>Dge I think all extlly</u>. Gave her 5/-. My head today is quite giddy all in consequence of my an'l pas'ns[149] and I feel very strange when walking, as if I was quite drunk, staggering. O how miserable I feel & find myself.

Sat 18th To Carmarthen. Handed two notes of £100 each due from Br Evan to me & the amount he refuses to me though he has £1,400 in Jones solicitor's hand at present. To Morris & Morris with instructions to proceed against him if he will not pay the amount before the middle of next week. Jones will soon be the owner of Nantegryd if he will continue to be an instrument of Montalembert's hands as he is at present. Evan is the greatest fool that ever existed, otherwise he would [do] what I bid him to do, that is to use the money from Jones to have nothing to do with him and Montalembert. Evan is awful to me at present. He cannot be worse when he will be served with a writ. He is incited to be exasperated with me by Montalembert.

---

149. Animal passions.

Sun 19th Took an oath before Evan Griffiths today (same as this day last year) that I would abstain from taking any intoxicating beverages from this day to the end of the present year. At home all day. Very warm. To Llanfair with Evan Griffiths at am.

Mon 20th At Llanfair all day preparing timber for the sale. To Tyssil Castle at dusk. Br Evan was here at night & he was desperate to me yet I kept from his sight. It seems that he had received a letter from my solicitor's for the payment of the £200. Also his creditors are sending their respective amounts and [he] throws all the problem upon me. In about 18 months he must either mortgage Nantegryd of make a sale of his stock and crop.

Wednes 22nd "Alas" Com Idt Ls with S't A. Dge almost to a <u>certainty</u> all <u>extlly</u>. Oh Oh what to do. Mother to Nantegryd yesterday but Evan not at home. He came down here and was terrible to me. I am sorry to think that he must be served with a writ before he will ever pay me. Much contrition all day for last night. O how I am buying a minute's pleasure to wail perhaps for years. I do not know at the present moment in what situation I am & what will come to light & if what I deserve will come there will be an end to me in this world at once.

Thurs 23rd At Llanfair cutting timber for the sale tomorrow. Brought two sacks full of the large ants and their nest from Llanfair & deposited them here by the old ruins in the wood as I find them very useful there in destroying insects that eat up the young leaves of the oaks in spring.

Fri 24th Llanfair timber sale. Had a very good sale notwithstanding all the cut at Coedfoel & Pantwen. Conducted myself well, Br Evan there & very drunk.

Sat 25th To Carmarthen. Rainy all the pm and never was it wanted more in Wales. Cattle generally has suffered from scarcity of grass. My flock had not half enough of grass.

Sun 26th To Dolgrogwys, idling at am. Chapel at pm. Found S't A again very cunning going to a place of worship in my absence when promised to stay at home as no one else at home. She is very wicked, take care of her.

Mon 27th To Llanfair & Tyssil Castle. Very hot, little rain fell as expected on Saturday, and none afterwards. Br Evan is fast using & spending the £1.400 left in the hands of Jones solicitor. He will in a few days be penniless. R'd all the R.[150]

Tues 28th Com Idt Ls with My Pen g r b n.[151] Very good appetite indeed. Very warm day. In the house myself most part of today. Had many hours quiet in my study. Br David is very useless & Talkative.

---

150. Rees is reading his rules again.
151. Rees has an ongoing and no doubt secret sexual relationship with Mary, who was a close neighbour, living within the same loop of the river Teifi as Dôl-llan.

Wednes 29th To Llanfair & Tyssil Castle. Also been to Pontwelly shop goods sale. Very hot day & quite exhausted myself. Jenkin came home from the Militia[152] yesterday.

Thurs 30th Late in bed. To Llanfair, R. Thomas Cribor here at am. To the above spot at pm. Cloudy day.

Fri 31st Little rain, the only fish that survived the long drought two years ago died in the canal today. It is almost quite dry. The river is not quite so small as it was in the summer of that year. There will be no fruit this year as all the blossoms that were open were killed by the frost.

JUNE 1861

Sat 1st The last of the mortgages of the money laid out by my father is put up to Br Evan today & in a few weeks it will all be spent. Now almost all the money saved by my father is within a few hundreds spent with the exception of the legacies of my sister and my late brother John. Br David is tolerably quiet for the last three days. Mother hastened to Tyssil Castle with the title Deeds of Tŷ Hen which is paid up today. Pd & Rd all the R.

Mon 3rd Last Saturday Mother succeeded in obtaining the Loan of £1,200, being the principle of the mortgage of Velingwm, of Evan at Nantegryd. One thousand of the above were lent to her on a Bond at 5 per cent & the remainder on an IOU. Evan during her short stay there abused her in every way whatever, calling her by every name. Montalembert was his legal advisor & Jones acted as a counsellor. The two latter gentlemen were ostensibly very reluctant for mother to concern in the affair. It is very wonderful how could any normal [person] suffer so much as Mother did on this occasion, one so haughty & insolent, the other, especially, Evan, proud & abusive. The day of retribution will soon come upon him.

Tues 4th "Alas" Com Idt Ls with S't A. <u>Dge</u> almost certainly <u>all Extlly</u>. It was last night. Sleepy and drowsy all day.

Wednes 5th The procession day of the Union Benefit.[153] Br Evan and his Serv't were the first at the union this morning & he & his servant were among the last that left there at night. Today his pockets were full of Gold & silver. This time 12 months, he will be almost penniless, as before that time he will squander all his money with the exception of Nantegryd *** [illeg]. David Lewis here making up Mother & other accounts. Fine day & very busy myself all day. Received a letter informing that Mr Evans Llaethlliw has obtained the Grant to raise a mortgage of £27,000 on his estate.

---

152. Jenkin Jones Thomas was an Ensign (October 1858) and later Lieutenant (March 1863) in the Cardiganshire Militia. He would have witnessed the unpopular decision to unite the Royal Cardigan Rifle Corps with the Brecknock amd Radnor Corps to form the Royal Cardigan Brecknock and Radnor Rifle Corps in 1861, which was to be reversed in 1867. The Militia trained at Aberystwyth. [Bryn Owen, *History f the Welsh Militia & Volunteer Corps, 1757–1908*, Bridge Books, Wrexham, 1995.]
153. Rees Thomas was a permanent auditor of the Union Benefit Club. The procession was invariably led by a brass band.

Thurs 6th To Llanfair at am. It was reported yesterday that Dr Evans, son of Mr Evans Mathry, was gone to be married to Anne Rees, daughter of David Rees, Tailor, Llandyssil. They both had gone to Newcastle Emlyn for some *** unwise [??] purpose and they returned same day. They are on every opportunity with each other and apparently there is great attachment between them.[154]

Fri 7th About the accounts of my relatives all day. Dr Davis called here, also Jones Solic't clerk & some others. Very hot & threatening thunder. Br Evan was served with three writs yesterday, one of which was from me for £200.

Mon 10th Received a letter from S't Betsy yesterday. An answer will be returned this week. S't A is very haughty. She has not the least memory when she puts anything from her own hands. The parlour keys were lost yesterday & were found by Hannah S't today. Other keys were lost before & never any found. Very warm dry weather. The river is quite as low now as it was the year before last.

Another binge begins on Tues 11th. He records having sex with his servant Anne on Wednesday 12th, is incapable for the following two days until the next entry:

Sat 15th Int. Idt Ls with S't A. Dge <u>intelly</u>. How I am at the end. O Lord what shall I do.

Mon 17th Still in a terrible state of bewilderment, partly owing to the unfavourable result from the last Idt Ls with S't A. She threatens that result will take place.

Tues 18th Terrible dreams all last night. Not a minutes rest. Today labouring under the <u>most awful mental depression</u> I ever had before, how happy should I be if I knew that my days are up. Very heavy rain yesterday evening, yet beautiful today, though sad and gloomy to me, & never will be better in future.

Wednes 19th Little better in body & spirit today, Also had little appetite. Very hot & sultry day. Out over the farm Yetwen & Frongoch. Mother at Tyssil Castle about Evan's affairs. He is the greatest fool that ever existed. Jones solicitor is fast & unfairly swallowing up his money & he will be soon penniless & eventually Jones intends coming soon the possession of Nantegryd.

Fri 21st Little Johnny here since when he came from school. Very hot & sultry at am, thunder & one good shower at pm. Dr Jones (at our request) visited Br David today & pronounced him in good health, though labouring under mental derangement. The reason of my sending for the Doctor was that David was walking over the country, i.e. by Llanfihangel Penrhiw, & was only quiet when taking his meals. He is for the last week or more out walking constantly and if anyone should say anything to him he either must go out of the way or to take blows.

---

154. David Rees, tailor, lived at 16 Bridge Street in 1851, when he was 36 and his daughter Anne was 7. There is no trace of this family in the 1861 census. [*1851 Census, Llandyssil.*]

Sat 22nd Out with the workmen all day. Very hot & sultry. Jenkin went to meet the two daughters of Llangunllo at Carmarthen on their way home. Today performed my religious duties by praying in Dolbante woods & then read all my rules, trusting in future to do so in earnestness & solemnity.

Wednes 26th David Lewis here yesterday & today – left at noon today. Capt Sheraton cuts his hay today. Very rainy at am yet cut hay from the swath to Llanfair. Under the impulse of the moment Com Idt Ls with A. Dge almost <u>certain all external</u>. What can be the cause of my morals so low as they are & have been this year. Quite time to repent & improve otherwise my fate is at hand.

JULY 1861

Thurs 4th Mother went in my Cart to Carmarthen yesterday. To Llanfair & Tyssil Castle. Br David is continually awfully angry when he comes to the house, cursing everyone & always threatening to hang Serv't Anne & very often he kicks & strikes her.

Sat 6th Rev'd T. Thomas Pantydefaid & the Rev'd Rees Jones Aberdar[155] here since last evening. Left both after breakfast today. Mother returned from Carmarthen today. "Alas" Come Idt Ls with S't A last night. Dge not certain whether some <u>intlly</u> or not (one more warning). Very rainy.

Sun 7th A large comet is visible since this day week.[156]

Mon 8th Mowing. (8 mowers). Brs Jenkin & Evan went down to hear the trial of the wife of the cobbler by whom he was poisoned.

Tues 9th To Tyssil Castle for Breakfast & on my coming home Com Idt Ls with My Pen grion. Good appetite. Very fine day, hay making all day.

Wednes 10th Out hay making all day. Went to hear a lecture at Ebenezer [Chapel] in the evening. "Alas" "alas" Com Idt Ls with S't A about 2 o'clock this morning. Dge <u>all extlly</u>.

Thurs 11th I was much frightened at 2 o'clock this morning by David [coming in] to my bedroom, however he had no wicked intentions as he was only coming for water to drink. Rainy today & had it not being [*sic*] our hay would come in easily. S't A breaks large quantities of earthenware.

Sun 14th Very unhappy all day solely owing to S't A. What made me to hire such a double faced Devil, but happily I have come to the resolution of dismissing her at the expiration of her year.

Mon 15th Very little talk between S't A & myself since yesterday morning. Very unhappy owing that I am obliged to allow S't Anne's intend[ed] to come here at night, otherwise she threatens to

---

155. Rees Jenkin Jones (1835–1924), Unitarian minister, schoolmaster, historian, and hymn-writer. [*Rev. John David Jones, B.D. (1898–1959), Carmarthen*, Welsh Biography Online.]
156. The Great Comet of 1861 (C/1861 J1 and 1861 II) was visible to the naked eye in the northern hemisphere from June 29. On June 30, 1861, the comet made its closest approach to the Earth and even cast shadows at night.

leave her service. Remember remember her. Fine day but threatening thunder all day. Mother & two seamstresses preparing bed hangings as Dr Lloyd, wife & children are coming to stay here for a few days.

Wednes 17th At home all day. Rainy, not much hope of having the hay in & now it begins to get mouldy. "Och" Com Idt Ls with My P-n g b n. Sleepy all day.

Thurs 18th To Evan Isaac[157] & between & shop y Jones got Dk. After coming home Com Idt Ls with S't A. No Disge I am almost certain.

Fri 19th Dr Lloyd, wife & children came here to stay a few days.

Sat 20th Dr Lloyd, wife & children went for a drive to Llandyssil.

Sun 21st Chapel at pm. Dr Lloyd officiated there, also at Llwynrhydowen in the morning.

Tues 23rd Very stormy day & rain. "Alas" "alas" Com Idt Ls with S't A. <u>Dchge</u> <u>almost</u> <u>certain</u> <u>all</u> <u>extlly</u>. Drank to elevation also last night. Br Evan at my mother's house today for cash. Idling with John Rees.

Wednes 24th Dr Lloyd, wife & children remained in the house all day; weather drizzling all day. Very drowsy myself. Br David hates staying in the house. Since Dr Lloyd's arrival he has been scolding so much, also singing for two nights.

Fri 26th Dr Lloyd, wife, two children & servant left for home this morning after been [*sic*] here for a week today. Been myself to Bwlchbychan today, buy a sheep for £2, also paying for a lamb ram which came from Aberglasney. Been all through the house, garden & farm. Been there for three hours.

Sat 27th Funeral of Dio Wynllan (went to it). He died last Thursday morning, aged 39 years. Budded some roses & plums. Sister here asking for the loan of money & was apparently in great need of same.

Sun 28th Chapel at pm. For a walk with John Rees Penalltgerdyn[158] at pm. Evans the master came over & not very sober after three days drinking.

Mon 29th Having the hay in and pretty good condition, many people assisted. Very windy & threatening rain. Awful rain just after we finished.

---

157. Evan Isaac (1823–1908), Llandysul, who kept a dairy from 1876 to 1885. [See H. R. Evans, *Ceredigion*, Vol. IV, No. 2, 1961.]
158. John Rees Penalltgerdyn: John Rees, aged 29, unmarried, butcher, lived with unmarried sister Mary, 24, one of Rees' sexual partners. [*1861 Census, Llanfihangel ar Arth.*]

Tues 30th To Llanfair & about the budding. Sister & her son here at pm. There is awful talk still about Jenkin's quarrel at Newcastle Emlyn summer with Mr Morris Blanevern about a horse which Jenkin bought & which Morris thought of buying. It was a very unfortunate affair to us as a family as we are awfully abused with Morris. Jenkin was Dk.

Wednes 31st David Lewis here all day, searching for receipts. Alas Com Idt Ls with My P y b n. Paid 2. 4—4 Shameful.[159] To the village. Drank four pints of porter & after coming [—] took two glasses of Gin, then Llanfair Dk & more Idt Ls with S't A but <u>no Dge</u> so no result expected. Hopeless state.

AUGUST 1861

Fri 2nd To Court Farm & Mr Hughes of Noyadd[160] relative to Llanfair affairs. Awful heartburn. Took two glasses of porter at Court.

Sat 3rd Very rainy at am, also at pm. Preparing lines of flies with John Rees for salmon fishing. At home all day, had it not been rainy this morning I would [have] gone to Carmarthen. David is drinking a good deal for the last seven days. Evan it seems has been ailing last week but is well now.

Tues 6th To Jones Sol'tr officer. There got Dk. Idt Ls with S't A. <u>No Dge no result</u>.

Wednesday 7th August marks the start of another alcoholic binge. That lasts until Sunday 11th, when the diary simple notes: "Bewildered".

Mon 12th Out in the woods by my poor self quite bewildered for my last drinking fit, from the effects there is ruin.

Wednes 14th Out in the woods by myself in such a state of mind that no mortal can describe. Pain in my back and side. I feel myself as if I had already departed this life, which I have made too miserable to continue. O God have pity upon me & pardon my sins. No repose yet at night, no not a single moment.

Thurs 15th Very low Spirited early in the morning & in the evening & have a very strange sensation in my head. Sometimes I feel giddy & at other times a burning sensation. Also I feel ardent desire for company. Mr Jones the cabinet[161] here putting the pictures up which he framed for Mother & myself. Rainy all day.

Fri 16th Mother & myself agreed to meet Mr & Mrs Sheraton at Llanfair so we did & Mrs Sh & Mother went all over the house examining everything to see what is wanted there. Mr Lewis

---

159. Unusually the diarist here inserts the code that he uses in the original manuscript to conclude an entry in the middle of the text. [See *Editor's Notes*.]
160. Thomas Hughes of Neuadd Fawr & Castell Du, Llanwnnen – an estate totalling more than 2,000 acres. [*Historic Cardiganshire Homes*, Brawdy Books, 2000.]
161. This could be one of several carpenters called Jones.

Cwmbychan[162] informed me that Bailiffs are distressing for the Wastfa[163] in five [farms] in the parish, who are name of Lewis, Penlan,[164] Penbont,[165] Cwmgwen[166] & myself. We are the chief defaulters & we pay.

Sat 17th Reading in bed till about 12 o'clock every night as I am too much in desponding to sleep.

Sun 18th At home all day. The wind blew a hurricane for about two hours at pm, accompanied with heavy rain. Killed a pig this afternoon before he would die from the effects, I have no doubt, of a blow on the head from someone (Hannah) I believe when getting there to have their meals at midday.

Mon 19th Blaendyffryn sale. Bought a few things there, never have I seen a sale so well attended with gentlemen and ladies before. Very much exhausted. Alas Com Idt Ls with S't A but thank [God] once more <u>all Dge was Extlly & certain of it this time</u>.

Tues 20th At Blaendyffryn sale about several things there today. Alas Com Idt Ls with S't A but think Dge all extlly & quite certain.

Wednes 21st Rent audit day at Llanfair. Fine day yet I feel myself somewhat not in my usual spirits. Moreover after the last debacle I hate being by myself especially at night. David has struck and kicked S't Anne several times this morning.

Thurs 22nd All day at Blaendyffryn sale. Bought a few things every day there and I am spending nearly 10s every day on beer.

Fri 23rd At Blaendyffryn sale. Came home early & before the sale finished. Mother is so foolish as paying Br Evan's creditors without any orders to do so from (***) [illeg], therefore she will have to be in there herself. Anne S't has come back again after been from there more than a week. Evan[167] went up at night to Tynrhos to fetch her himself after sending many messengers [to] beg of her to come. First she refused till Evan would come personally so he did go. David is rather ferocious this week again.

Sat 24th Having the clover hay in, also reaping and binding corn. Paid Mother yesterday £50 on account of her annuity. She thought that I wanted to her to sign a receipt for the whole amount. I think that she is rather suspicious of my honesty & uprightness. However I have a calm conscience, well knowing that I never cheated her of a farthing. She is now very angry with me.

---

162. I believe this refers to Lewis Evans, 35, of Cwmbychan, a 65-acre farm. [*1861 Census, Llanfihangel ar Arth.*]
163. Gwestfa – a property tax.
164. James Thomas, 48. Penlan is a farm of 84 acres. [*1861 Census.*]
165. Not known in Llanfihangel ar Arth parish.
166. Evan Evans, a 73-year-old widower, cattle dealer and farmer of 120 acres just south of Pencader. [*1861 Census.*]
167. Evan Thomas, the diarist's youngest brother.

Photograph of Gwilym Marles.
(Image with signature from Lloyd Letters*).*

Sketch of Rev'd David Lloyd, principal
of Carmarthen College.
(From Lloyd Letters*, edited by George Eyre Evans).*

Dr Henry Harries Davies.
(One of Rees Thomas' doctors).

Hiring Fair in Wales, 1853 (old print).

The Market Place, Carmarthen, 1860 (old print).

Market scene, Cardiganshire (old print).

Bridge Street, Newcastle Emlyn.

Haymaking on a Llandyssul farm.
(Old postcard, courtesy of Thomas Lloyd).

Haymaking at Blaendyffryn.
(Old postcard, courtesy of Thomas Lloyd).

Diary, November 1860.
(Photograph: Steve Dubé, courtesy of Pembroke Record Office).

Diary: December 1860–January 1861.
(Photograph: Steve Dubé, courtesy of Pembroke Record Office).

Pantydefaid Chapel (old postcard).

Rees Thomas, gravestone.
(Photograph: Steve Dubé).

Heenan the prize fighter (see page 77).

Blondin the tightrope walker (see page 82).

The International Exhibition in Kensington Gardens, London (see page 81).

REGISTRATION DISTRICT DOSBARTH COFRESTRU }	NEWCASTLE IN EMLYN		
1865 DEATH in the Sub district of MARWOLAETH yn Is-ddosbarth } Llandyssul		in the yn	Counties of Cardigan & Carmarthen

No. Rhif	1 When and where died Pryd a lle y bu farw	2 Name and surname Enw a chyfenw	3 Sex Rhyw	4 Age Oed	5 Occupation Gwaith	6 Cause of death Achos marwolaeth	7 Signature, description and residence of informant Llofnod, disgrifiad a chyfeiriad yr hysbysydd	8 When registered Pryd y cofrestrwyd	9 Signature of registrar Llofnod y cofrestrydd
251	Seventh November 1865 Dolellan Llanfihangelararth	Rees Thomas	Male	42 years	Landed Proprietor	Neuralgia of the Knee Joint and asthenia from Malaria Certified	Joshua Evans In Attendance Golden Mortar Llandyffsil	Ninth November 1865	Edward Evans Registrar

Death certificate: Rees Thomas.

REGISTRATION DISTRICT DOSBARTH COFRESTRU }	NEW CASTLE IN EMLYN		
1860 DEATH in the Sub district of MARWOLAETH yn Is-ddosbarth } Llandyssul		in the yn	Counties of Cardigan & Carmarthen

No. Rhif	1 When and where died Pryd a lle y bu farw	2 Name and surname Enw a chyfenw	3 Sex Rhyw	4 Age Oed	5 Occupation Gwaith	6 Cause of death Achos marwolaeth	7 Signature, description and residence of informant Llofnod, disgrifiad a chyfeiriad yr hysbysydd	8 When registered Pryd y cofrestrwyd	9 Signature of registrar Llofnod y cofrestrydd
84	Eleventh February 1860 Llanfair Llandyssil	Thomas Thomas	Male	43 years	Landed Proprietor	Dropsy Certified	Rees Thomas Present at the Death Dolellan Llanfihangelararth	Fifteenth February 1860	Edward Evans Registrar

Death certificate: Thomas Thomas.

Sun 25th Chapel at am. With John Rees[168] Serv't Evan[169] & Dio Ffynnonbwla[170] to Llanfair. Remained two hours in Pentybach. Returning pottery & pots. Quite drunk when arrived home. Egged ourselves uncommonly, or at least I did. It was rather cold & had some rain on our way home. S't A went out for a short time from chapel at Pantydefaid.

Fri 30th David Lewis & myself about Llanfair accounts. "Alas" Com Idt Ss with S't Anne last night. Dge almost certainly extlly. I sincerely trust this will be the last time.

SEPTEMBER 1861

Mon 2nd To the funeral of Shane y Crydd,[171] the sister of the Rev'd John James Gellionnen. Rev'd T. Thomas Pantydefaid & his friend Rev'd John Davis Dancoed here tonight.

Wednes 4th Funeral of Dr Jones Lodge's wife.[172] It was about one third of that of my brother John. Took a stroll with the gun up to Dolgrogwys but I think there are no partridges on the land.

Sat 7th Served with a writ of summons from Ianto Gof.[173]

Mon 9th To Jones office at pm relative to Mother's affairs. Sister here at pm. Very active at present in finding evidence against the Bill of Ianto Gof against Mother.

Tues 10th Rev'd T. Thomas Pantydefaid [here] since last night. Out shooting with Amphlett & him over the Farm & Graig & Wernmackwith. Shot 5 Braces of Partridge, hare & a rabbit. Rev'd T. Thomas here over the night. Drank 3 glasses of porter at Wernmackwith.

Wednes 11th Rev'd T. Thomas left for home after Breakfast this morning. David is in a rage all day & very restless & quarrelsome.

Thurs 12th To Llanybyther meeting appeal and "Alas" after coming home Com Idt Ls with S't A. Dge all (almost to a certainty) Extlly. Remember to dismiss her next November otherwise I repent for not doing so.

Wednes 18th At Jones office almost all day taking down the depositions of the witnesses with Jones. Awful anxiety & trouble for the issue of tomorrow. Took about a pint of Beer last night and under affects Com Idt Ls with S't A. Dge I am almost sure all Extlly.

---

168. John Rees, Penalltgerdyn.
169. Evan Davies, 25, a farm servant at Dôl-llan.
170. David Titus, 40, a carpenter living at nearby Fynnonbwla.
171. Jane. *Crydd* = cobbler or shoemaker. Jane Jones, a shoemaker's widow, aged 73, lived at Upper Barley Mount in Llandysul. [*1861 Census, Llandyssil.*]
172. Dr John Jones, surgeon, aged 41, was married to Eliza, also 41. [*1861 Census, Llandyssil.*]
173. Ianto is a diminutive of the first name Evan and a *gof* is a blacksmith. There are two possibilities in the 1861 census for Llandysul – Evan Edwards, 45 of Llaingignach in Llandysul village and Evan Rees, 44, listed as living and working at Glanrhyd smithy just on the Cardiganshire side of the bridge at Llanfihangel ar Arth.

Thurs 19th The law suit between Ianto Gof & myself was tried at Newcastle Emlyn County Court today. The verdict was in my favour. Half DK so as usual Com Idt Ls with S't A. <u>Dge quite certain all Extlly</u>.

Tues 24th Today I was such a fool to grieve in anticipation of the time that my S't A was leaving. And in order to be more of a fool drank till Half DK, again to make everything worse then Com Idt Ls with S't A but thank [God] <u>no Dge</u>.

Thurs 26th At Llanfair all of us all day. Capt Sheraton's[174] head Girl was there today. Beautiful day.

Fri 27th At Llanfair taking an inventory of all the Household furniture & other articles. There from 8am to 10.30pm. Very stormy late in the evening.

Sat 28th At Llanfair six carts loaded with Capt Sheraton's articles came there. No stock came yet. Mother because rather low spirited & touchy to me when seeing other persons things coming there.

Sun 29th Very showery weather, at home all day. Mr & Mrs Griffiths Dolgrogwys here all pm, also Mr Edward Evans Abercerdyn.[175] Br David is still in a rage.

Mon 30th At Llanfair most part of the day before noon. David was still in such a rage that he kicked S't A & got hold of Mother by her arms & threw her down on the pavement by the Pump & after I came home a quarrel took place between S't A & David the Steward, as we call Br David's Keeper,[176] about giving Sob [?] to Br David. Heard yesterday that Evans Llaethlliw[177] & his wife are at Court Farm both as jolly as ever. The Tivy is closed against Salmon fishing with nets today. Ceffyl Pren is to be carried the third time tonight to the man of Pwllebryn[178] for beating his wife. Many police went up to stop them.[179]

OCTOBER 1861

Tues 1st Com Idt Ss [last] night with S't A when she had mthly m n-s. Dge all Extlly I think but not certain. To the sale of Court Farm, conducted myself well.

---

174. Capt Sheraton is going to rent Llanfair mansion.
175. Edward Evans, Abercerdin: Aged 42, Registrar of births & deaths and a farmer of 60 acres. Unmarried and lives with his brother Evan. [*1861 Census, Llandyssil.*]
176. This is probably David Davies, aged 69, employed as a farm labourer at Dôl-llan.
177. The Rev'd Evan Evans.
178. Jenkin Jones, aged 36, a farmer of 151 acres at Pwllerbryn. His wife is Mary, aged 47. [*1861 Census, Llandyssil.*]
179. *Ceffyl Pren*: literally "wooden horse", a sort of vigilante justice on people adjudged by common consent to have done wrong. Policing and suppressing the *ceffyl pren* was one of the main briefs of the new rural police, established in the wake of the Rebecca Riots. During the closing years of the nineteenth century, the Chief Constable of Cardiganshire Constabulary could comment that the practice was no more. [*Ceredigion: Journal of the Cardiganshire Antiquarian Society*, Vol. 11, nos. 1-4 (1989–1992).]

Wednes 2nd At Llanfair all the am, to the village at pm. John Evans shoe maker[180] here at night for two hours. Capt Sheraton & his wife came to Llanfair to sleep at night, being the first time.

Thurs 3rd At home all day. Capt Sheraton of Llanfair here at am. First time he stated that he was not willing to stand by the agreement & consequently we both rather lost our good humour. However I went over there in the evening again & we were pretty well to each other.

Fri 4th Very sleepy every day, especially after dinner. Capt Wallop[181] & Amphlett came home by here after being fishing complaining that Capt Sheraton had stopped them fishing when they were on the land of Farm. He supposed them on Graig land & then Capt Sheraton in the right to stop them. Br David is daily in a rage. He has gone off singing and counting in a strange language a long time ago. I think that he is getting gradually more passionate. The Tailors are sewing a snigget [?] to put on the large parlour floor. Wrote a letter to Old S't By.[182]

Tues 8th Fishing up the river with Amphlett all am. No sign of a salmon. There were many policemen with their Capt at Llandyssil Alltyrodyn Arms last night again to prevent Ceffyl Pren.

Wednes 9th At Llanfair all day almost. Been to the village last night at the request of Mother with writ which Mitchell[183] sent to Br Evan at the suit of David Williams Kings Head[184] for £135.17.6 asserting to be due from Evan for spirits. I understand Jones Llandyssil to enter an appearance with the view of having a Bill of Particulars from him. Alas Com Idt Ls with S't Anne. Dge all externally almost to a certainty.[185] Thank God for November being so near to dismiss her.

Thurs 10th To Llanfihangel fair. Came home early, called by Llanfair. Mother was there. Asked S't Evan[186] & Anne whether they would stay with me another year. The former said that he would be having exorbitant wages & the latter that she intended going to her brothers in England.[187]

Fri 11th To Llwyncroes, Mr Jones & to Pencarreg fair. Hired S't Evan again for the ensuing year. S't Anne refuses to stay, saying that she is going to her brothers to Yorkshire. I do not wish S't Hannah to stay. I am happy to state that I have not taken a drop too much yesterday or today. Received a letter from S't By yesterday. Weather rough & stormy.

Sat 12th To Llanfair & Llandyssil late at night & after coming home Com Idt Ls with S't Anne. Dge I Presume all Extlly.

---

180. John Evans, shoemaker: Lived at Upper Barley mount. Aged 40, and employed three men. [*1861 Census, Llandyssil.*] It is exactly one month since Evans buried his wife.
181. Barter Wallop, aged 46, born London, was a lodger at the Old Black Lion, Llandysul, at the time of the census in April, 1861. Amphlett lived next door.
182. Still unable to forget his former servant.
183. Evidently a solicitor.
184. David Williams kept the Kings Head Inn with his widowed mother Hannah, aged 68, and his widowed sister, aged 40. [H. R. Evans, *Ceredigion*, Vol. IV, No. 2, 1961.]
185. Underlining here as elsewhere is the diarist's own.
186. Evan Davies, aged 25.
187. Just one day after again resolving to dismiss her, he asks his servant Anne to stay.

Sun 13th Wind blowing a hurricane today, though not much rain like yesterday. At home all day. For a walk by Dolgrogwys & Ffynnonbwla, very low Spt. The children of the latter place captured a polecat & he bit them severely, think he was my lost ferret.

Mon 14th To Llandyssil (the office) relative to Br E affairs. I am for the last month so drowsy that I am obliged to sleep for an hour or more after every meal I take.

Tues 15th DK several glasses of Beer there till I got into a state of elevation. Alas Com Idt Ls with S't A. <u>Dge all Extlly</u> almost to a certainty.

Wednes 16th To the sale at Highmead.[188] Desponding & unwell from the effects of yesterday. My morals are gone ten times worse than they ever were before. It is a thing of very great importance that Serv't A is going away this year. Weather beautiful.

Thurs 17th At home all day with the exception of the time I went for a walk over Dolgrogwys & through the fields above Ffynnonbwla, where I laid down by the side of a hedge commanding a fine view of my old native place where I spent the best time of my life & the reminiscences of which came fast upon my memory & imparted the highest pleasure. Laid about 2 hours and unfortunately caught a severe cold.

Fri 18th Serv't Evan with my plough & horses at Llanfair today, being the third day this week. Suffering from severe cold. In the house all the pm. Bad heartburn & pain in my chest. David is still hale & hearty.

Sat 19th Once more Com Idt Ls with S't A. <u>Dge all Extlly</u> to a certainty. Very bad cold still. For a walk to Dolgrogwys making enquiries for Servant Girls.

Mon 21st Funeral of Evan Ffynnonliwelyn, an old man of 83.[189] Very rainy. Looking out for Servant Girls for the ensuing year. S't A is now quite willing to stay for another year but she does not say so plainly, yet it can be gathered from her conversation today. However I hope it is too late as I have already sent for one, if she will come as I hope.

Tues 22nd Once more, and I hope for the last time, Com Idt Ls with S't A. Dge all <u>Extlly</u> almost quite certain. Hired Hannah, present maid of Shopnewydd, to be my head servant for the coming year.[190] Anne, my present Serv't, seems to repent most awfully for not staying when asked her to do.

Wednes 23rd S't Anne is crying all day after I told her that I have hired one for her.

---

188. Highmead Mansion, Llanybydder.
189. Possibly the father of David Jones, 46, farmer of the 75-acre Ffynnonlywelyn.
190. Hannah Jones, aged 25, unmarried, born in Llangeler. [*1861 Census, Llandyssil.*]

Thurs 24th Shooting rabbits & ferreting all day with Watty & Dio Ffynnonbwla. Killed 21. Very wet day. To Dolgrogwys, Dk there a half bottle of resin wine & some Beer till half gone. After coming home Com Idt Ls with S lly Plgrhu.[191] Dge <u>all Extlly</u>.

Fri 25th Unwell as usual the next day. Did nothing today but lying on the sofa. Oh how lavish my time, most disgracefully.

Sun 27th Com Idt with S't A twice. Dge all extlly both times. It took place last night. At home all day, very low Spt & poorly.

Mon 28th To Carmel to make out land for the graveyard. Fine weather, cold wind from the East. To Llandyssil at pm. S't A was offered to go to Vairdre fach either in the capacity of Cook or dairy maid. She is, poor girl, very sorry to leave here after having an offer many a time to stay. Gwrtheyrn & Pengallt Llanfair were lighted or had fires on in consequence of a squabble between Shane Pensingrig[192] & her two sisters about 2 Sundays ago. I went up to Gwrtheyrn & collared some with threats of further prosecutions if they were not immediately parted & go home. They got so frightened & they all left their bonfires, running here and there like wild beasts & throwing their candles down & thus I frustrated their attempt in the bud of thinking of Ceffyl Pren in this neighbourhood. After that bonfires were to be seen on different hills about here tonight.

Tues 29th At Llanfair & Bridgend new house. A good of talk today about the frightened boys running last night like wild beasts after my presence in their midst. Ceffyl Pren is threatened for hardly anything in this part at present. Br Evan & some boy were fined yesterday of £2 each at the Petty Sessions for being instigators at the Pwllebryn Ceffyl Pren.

Thurs 31st At home all day except at Pen pwll hiring a servant girl. Sister here at pm & it seems that her state with Davis is a most miserable one. I advised her to leave him. David has been just the same this month as the last three or four months. My moral character has been low to the extreme in the month which now closes for ever. I have made a new rule for my guidance on the path of temperance & [it] is to be observed from tomorrow & I trust to the end of my days. Idt Ls with S't A. Dge all extlly.

NOVEMBER 1861

Fri 8th Com Idt Ls with S't A last night. <u>Dge all extlly</u>. Sleepy and drowsy as usual. Hard frost. Mangels all housed. 28 loads & 2 of carrot.

Sun 10th At home all day. Very showery & cold. William Davies Gilfachwen[193] & his brother here to dinner. S't Anne been to Ebenezer at pm, last Sunday for her here[194] Good Girl. Anne Nant-

---

191. S lly = Sally = Sarah Jones, aged 27, of Plygyrhiw, daughter, spinster and housekeeper of John Samuel, 76, mason. [*1861 Census.*]
192. Shane Pensingrig is Jane Jones, aged 40, wife of David Jones, also 40, an agricultural labourer. They had three daughters aged one to 14. [*1861 Census, Llandyssil.*]
193. William Davies of Gilfachwen Ucha, aged 34, a farmer of 105 acres employing three labourers. [*1861 Census, Llandyssil.*]
194. He expects her to be gone by next Sunday, but his feelings remain confused.

egryd[195] giving her depositions to me relative to Williams King's Head Bill. Evan Griffiths here. Br Evan is drinking hard.

Wednes 13th Mr Amphlett & myself shooting pheasants. Shot 3 & 1 hare & 3 rabbits. They are intended for presents. S't Anne in a worse temper than I ever saw her before. Refused to bring dinner to table before Amphlett & myself. To Jones office at dusk. David is very angry today, walking & no minute's rest but for his meals. Weather very wet & cold. David Nantygragen pensioner[196] is on a visit to Nantegryd. Evan is not coming often down to the village now.

Fri 15th Com Idt Ls with S't A. Dge all extlly. I am now almost certain that this will be the last time for her. Mr Amphlett & myself shooting. Sent to Carmarthen tonight by my cart the following presents of game: Dr Lloyd,[197] brace of pheasants; Mr Smith ditto; Rev'd Titus Evans, one pheasant & hare; to Mr Spurrell,[198] one pheasant & a rabbit. I am informed that Br Evan has been so foolish as to hire David Jones pensioner Nantygragen as a Steward at Nantegryd for a year.

Mon 18th The new servants Hannah & Rachel entered their service today. Anne is leaving tomorrow & she is awfully repenting for saying that she could not stay for another year.

Tues 19th S't Anne left today. I truly feel much grief after her. DK to elevation & when in that state mixed with grief Com Idt Ls with S't Hh.[199] <u>Dge all Extlly</u>. My anxiety today is very great owing Iant Gof law suit against Mother.

Wednes 20th My Poor bitch of the name of Swallow was accidentally shot yesterday by Dr Evans while shooting here. Today I have determined to live a better life than I have hitherto done this year. Prayed in the woods of Dolbank and read all my rules.

Thurs 21st To the County Court at the suit of Ianto Gof against Mother, being an adjourned case. Ianto's claim this time was instantly objected to by the new judge because it had no dates on it. The cost of the trial before this time is to be borne by Ianto & he must pay that expense before he can proceed again in this case, so Ianto was beaten every time yet.

Sun 24th My thoughts are pointed to S't A all day. Have somehow or other [a] little love for her & which daily attacks me with more or less power. Only trusting it will soon be over & that I shall be able to concentrate my thoughts on a more worthy & refined object of attachment.

Mon 25th Br Evan at Llanfihangel Petty Sessions to answer to summons for non-payment of wages to his Shepherd boy.[200] Jones Soli'tr appeared for him and he got free.

---

195. Anne Oliver 35, dairy maid at Nantegryd. A native of Llangeler.

196. David pensioner, alias Serg't Jones Nantygragen. The Jones family lived at Nantygragen in Llanfihangel ar Arth parish for 30 years from the first census, but there was no record of a David Jones.

197. Rev'd David Lloyd.

198. William Spurrell (1813–1889), printer, publisher and local historian, whose business operated from King Street, Carmarthen for nearly 100 years from 1841. [Joyce & Victor Lodwick, *The Story of Carmarthen*, 1953.]

199. New servant, new sexual partner. Hannah only in service for one day.

200. John Davies, aged 9.

Tues 26th Raining in torrents, wind from the South, continued from dusk last night to 10 o'clock today without interruption. Tivy began overflowing its banks but not amounting to flood yet. It contained more water than at any time yet this year. I was informed by a letter from Jones that the trial between Williams & Br Evan will not proceed before next July & I am very glad, hoping that we will agree before the time comes.[201]

Wednes 27th Alas Com Idt Ls with S't Hh. Dge all Extlly. I think this will be the last as I intend to turn another leaf next month.

Fri 29th Sister here yesterday evening. It is really very uncomfortable on her as it possibly can ever be on woman. No servants as Drunken Davis will not pay any. No fuel or anything hardly in the house as every farthing that comes in Davis spends it on drink & is behaving very cruel to her in every way whatever. I do not allow her to complain about him to me as she refused to part with him on any account. Br Evan here at pm Drunk and very noisy. I did not see him. He drinks now more than he ever used to do, a gallon of Brandy & Gin goes up from the druggist every day.

Sat 30th Posting all day to dusk, then reading. David Nantygragen, alias Serg't Jones, still at Nantegryd. Evan & himself drinking or somehow or other consuming a gallon of Spirits every day. He, the pensioner, is there in the capacity of a Steward & account Keeper. From today I intend reforming my moral Conduct & to read the Rules every morning & pray regularly twice a week in the woods.

DECEMBER 1861

Sun 1st Chapel at am. Dry windy day. Received a letter [from] Annie, being the first this quarter, and there was expression of sorrow for my removing her & her sister from Chester school this Xmas.

Mon 2nd I have still much attachment for my old S't A & often by myself I play nocturnal interviews with her.

Wednes 4th Posting Llanfair accounts from sunrise to sunset. David is getting in a rage after supper every night of late in consequence of us hiding his shoes to prevent his going his rounds after night. He left about 9 tonight in his slippers & lost them from here to the farm. The night was pitched dark and stormy. Mother in a rage all day since yesterday as she is always accustomed to after being down with Jenkin at Tyssul Castle.

Thurs 5th Down on foot to Blaendyffryn to see at a distance the meet & hunt of the Tivyside Hounds. A fox was started at Alltycavan and was lost by Penpistill. Jenkin was there on horseback & another of his horses under Capt Wallop there. Mother went to Carmarthen and is coming home on Saturday. Beautiful day. Dk 3 glasses of Br at home and so Com Idt Ls with S't Hh. Dge all Extlly so no result.

---

201. Claims by David Williams Kings Head for £135.17.6 allegedly due from Evan for spirits. See entry for October 9, 1861.

Sat 7th To Pantydefaid & Llanfair. Mother came home from Carmarthen. I am getting on much better than I ever anticipated with Serv't Hannah & really I do not feel the loss of Anne half so much as I thought. About 30 fruit trees came home from Bristol today to be planted in the new orchard at Cae Suserne [?]. Next week there are 8,000 two year seedlings whitethorns come home again, the cost about 5/- per thousand. Then and at the same time there are about 10 standard roses.

Sun 8th Chapel at pm. Very heavy showers. To the Tabernacl at 6 o'clock hearing the chief preacher of the Methodist Jones Blaenannerch.[202] He began his sermon with a voice so low that he was inaudible & when about the middle he began bellowing out that he could be heard for a mile. His sermon was descriptive of our state hereafter and our souls when we die, all nonsense.

Mon 9th Planting fruit trees I had from Bristol. To Llanfair at pm. Had a long conversation with Capt. We went up to shut Cefn Llanfair stones to prevent the Fox from going in tomorrow as the meet is to be at Llanfair. Terrific thunder at noon and followed by heavy showers. There is thunder every day almost & it rains almost every day & very wet.

Tues 10th To the meet of Brynog Fox hounds at Llanfair & there also Dk one glass of Brandy & it took very much effects upon me. Came home & took to drinking.

Wednes 11th Int in bed all day. Awfully rainy. The Tivy was about 12 o'clock tonight larger than it has been in the memory of any living inhabitant. The loss it made in uprooting trees is awful.

Fri 13th The Tivy is still larger today again than it has been before with my memory.[203] Hf Drunk myself.

Sat 14th The Tivy recedes very slow. I am truly bewildered this time.

Sun 15th My Uncle (Mr Rees Thomas) Ffoshelig died very suddenly this morning while preparing himself to go to chapel. The cause of death was an attack of apoplexy.[204]

Mon 16th With Mother at Ffoshelig. It seems that my Uncle died from disease of the heart as he had several slight attacks this week previous though he immediately recovered from each attack and was Saturday before his death at Llanwnen fair. Anne & Mary came home from Chester school last Friday. They are both through the instigation of Jenkin furious to me. Saw Anne as I was going by Tyssil Castle today.

Tues 17th At home all day, very unwell from pain in my chest. Been to the office for some time last night. Brother Evan impounded the milk cows of Evan Rees Bank Rhenbont[205] in the yard of

---

202. Rev'd John Jones (1807–1875).
203. The biggest flood in Llandysul for 70 years, with four feet of water between Abercerdin and Penpwll. [W. J. Davies, *Hanes Plwyf Llandyssul*, J. D. Lewis, 1896.]
204. Uncle Rees Thomas Ffoshelig: Rees Thomas, aged 64, farmer of 200 acres employing one labourer. Married to Anne, 68. Household also included two carters, a dairy maid and two housemaids.
205. Evan Rees, Bank Rhenbont: Evan Rees, 36, farmer of 50 acres at Banc Henbont on the banks of the river Clettwr near Capel Dewi, and a neighbour of Evan Thomas at Nantegryd.

Porth last night & they are still there today. Sent my cart with Mother for the Grave of my Uncle, also to carry Stones for the farm from Penpwll.

Wednes 18th Funeral of my late Uncle Ffoshelig & it was a very large funeral. He was buried at Llandyssil church yard according to the intense wish of his widow & as contrary as anything to the oft repeated wish of the now dead about a fortnight before his death. He said to a friend that nothing could cause him more grief than knowing that he would be buried at Llandyssil. Rev'd T T[206] here and others.

Fri 20th With David Lewis about the acc't all day. The children of Llanfair have all been here at pm except David, who is out on horseback after the Brynog hounds with Jenkin. Neither Anne nor Mary appeared on any good terms with me, both had a very sulky look. Com Idt Ls with S't Hh. Dge all <u>extlly</u>. Hh has been courting with the youth of Gorrig and another by this week. The hounds today hunted about Llanfair but found nothing. Very fine day. Little frost.

Sat 21st To Llanfair at am. The Tivy in its last incomparable inundation came to the canal under the old orchard at Llanfair and covered all the new planted orchard in the meadow.

Mon 23rd To Pantydefaid, intensely cold & penetrating wind. My thoughts are very often dwelling on on S't A.

Tues 24th Labouring under a great desponding all day, my thoughts still dwelling on S't A. Com Idt Ls with S't Hh. <u>Dge all Extlly.</u>

Wednes 25th Messrs Evans Pistill & the Druggist & him shooting at am. Very little game found. Shot 3 pheasants I woodcock & 5 rabbits. All the children of Llanfair come here to dinner (to Mother), told the eldest 3 that they ought to have come to explain their school bills. They left soon and were very angry with me. Mother had a goose for dinner and I had a share of it. Hard frost last night.

Fri 27th Alas Com Idt Ls with S't H. <u>Dge all Extlly</u>. David Lewis here all day and night. DK to elevation.

Sat 28th To Nantegryd with Mr Jones solicitor, taking the depositions of the Servants down relative to Williams Kings Head law suit. Hard frost and very cold.

Sun 29th At home all day. Took a walk by the riverside as far as Ffynnonbwla. Very chilly all day, also misty. David Lewis left here at noon. My night thoughts are particularly centred in Old S't A.

Tues 31st Rev'd Titus Evans here about the accounts between Jenkin & Llanfair & myself. Also Mrs Evans & her children here.

---

206. Rev'd Thomas: Thomas Thomas (1824–1908) (no relation), Minister of Pantydefaid Chapel.

1862 JANUARY

Jan'y 1st Wednes More children & a few grown people have been here today than for some years before. I was in the room all day examining the accounts with Mr T. Evans.[207] Frosty weather.

Thurs 2nd Rev'd T. Evans here still about the accounts and none yet finished. He left at noon. Mr Pryse Glangwilly[208] died very suddenly yesterday from the disease of the heart. Fine day & no frost.

Fri 3rd To Llanfair marking timber to be cut. Wernmacwith fishing was let to Messrs Amphlett & Wallop for £1.10.0 and a salmon a year. Mother had very much hatred towards me somehow or other on account of the children, yet that hatred is suppressed hitherto but she could not do it for a long time.

Tues 7th David Lewis here. Went to Mr Jones office about Williams law suit. Joined Jones & Amphlett to abstain from all intoxicating drink for 12 calendar months. We drank a good deal of Beer tonight as tomorrow our pledge is to be observed.

Wednes 8th Awful headache all day. Incapacitated myself to do any good all day from the effects of drink at Amphlett's house last night till 12 o'clock & Alas Com Idt Ls with Hh. Dge all <u>Extlly</u>.

Thurs 9th David Lewis & myself preparing D's accounts all day. To Mr Jones office at night respecting Williams law suit. Fine day. Br Evan had an awful attack of illness last Sunday but he soon recovered from his fit. M[209] is out with me now and is at Tyssul Castle today.

Fri 10th To Mr Jones office & to Nantegryd with him drilling the witnesses. Unwell.

Sat 11th Alas after I went over to Jones office yesterday at noon, drunk several bottles of ginger wine with Amphlett till I got drunk. When entering the coracle at Penpwll when coming home, fell into the river and got all wet, then came round the bridge. O what a talk there is today about me. Mitchell gave me a notice of withdrawal of the law suit to Jones about noon today so it will not go further this time. Anne Nantegryd[210] was down in the village tonight quite drunk and the new band paraded the streets & chaired Jones. Spent a lot of money myself on this law suit affair. Spent 6..0..0. Idt with S't H. <u>Dge all extlly</u>. Quite out of my senses.

Sun 12th At home all day labouring under much mental anguish, yes till I am quite wild. Mother is much out with me. O how miserable I am & Oh I wish I would die.

---

207. Rev'd Titus Evans.
208. John Lloyd Price (b.1803) of Glangwili, Llanllawddog, the magistrate that Rees Thomas went to see on 21 September 1860 after youths stole apples and broke branches in his orchard.
209. Mother.
210. Anne Oliver, dairy maid at Nantegryd.

Mon 13th Old Xmas day.[211] Writing long & dreary day, awful despondency at time, my thoughts dwelling unflingngly [*sic*] on old S't A, worse today than any other day. Very late in getting up this morning. Watty & Dio Carpt ferreting, captured 7 rabbits.

Tues 14th Br Evan here & presented me with a fat goose. Anne Thomas Llanfair[212] here. Had a little conversation with her. Not nearly recovered myself after the last fit of DK ness.

Wednes 15th Rent audit day of Llanfair. It was here for the first time, & I hope the last time too. Serv't Evan with my team ploughing at Llanfair with Capt Sheraton.

Thurs 16th At home all am. To Vairdre fach timber sale at pm. M[213] gone to Nantegrhyd & came home tonight again. Cold high wind from the East. My thoughts still take a very often flight to the bosom of my old S't A. No 3 consecutive hours yet passed without the above taking place. "Shame" Com Idt Ls with S't H. <u>Dge all Extlly</u>.

Fri 17th To Llanfair at am. "Alas" drunk a glass of Br mixed with water owing to despondency in consequence of last night. Dry and high wind blowing from the East. Very cold.

Sun 19th Chapel at am. Very cold. Idling all pm, no reading of anything. M has very great enmity for me now for the last fortnight. J[214] is her favourite at present & there is no wonder as his duplicity is unlimited. My mind dwelling upon the abuse of the 12 & consequently Com om.[215]

Mon 20th To Court respecting the children. Intensely cold. Sister here & also Anne Thomas.

Wednes 22nd Mother has been tried by Mitchell at the suit of Ianto Gof with copy of Ianto Gof's bill with dates attached thereto to Jones office with the suit bill last night.

Thurs 23rd Rev'd T. Thomas here since last night. Left early this morning. Went to Llandyssil at pm. The goods of Hannah Porth were sold under execution at the suit of Williams Kings Head.[216]

Fri 24th In company with Evan Dolgrogwys out in his meadow all am. Also seeing if the Fox hounds would come down there from Bwlchbychan. David, Anne & Jenkin went to the meet. Very windy & showery day. I feel myself very happy when walking by the side of hedges, especially on a windy day. To the concert at Llandyssil at night.

Sat 25th To Mr Jones office at am. Not well, and awful despondency all day. With Evan Dolgrogwys over Bank farm at pm. Shot 7 rabbits. Fine day. Br Evan here at dusk and was in a very

---

211. *Calan Hen*. Llandysul, along with some other parts of Wales, continued to mark the "old new year" after the "lost eleven days" of the switch from the Julian to the Gregorian calendar in September 1752.
212. His niece.
213. Mother.
214. Jenkin.
215. The diarist's "12" rules crop up again. Com om is an example of a code that the editor finds indecipherable.
216. Hannah Evans, a 53-year-old widow, who lived with her niece Mary Jones, aged 18, a house servant and a lodger Rees Rees, aged 29, a school teacher. [*1861 Census, Llandyssil*.]

bad temper. He is about spending all his money and will soon have to spend & squander Nant-egryd in the bargain.

Mon 27th David Lewis here at Llanfair accounts. Heard with Dd. Lewis today that old S't A was courting her former partner. That affected me so much that I became most miserable & low spirited all day.

Tues 28th To Llandyssil with Mr Jones last night till 3 this morning. I was first with Amphlett & Jones. Very rainy when coming home this morning and after Com Idt with S't Hh. <u>Dge</u> none <u>at all</u>. David Lewis here & we both DK to excess. Divulged all the attachment I had for old S't A to David Lewis.

Wednes 29th David Lewis & myself about Llanfair & David accounts all [day], also preparing for going to the County Court tomorrow to appear on behalf of Mother against Ianto Gof Bill. Sent Evan for witness today.

Thurs 30th To Newcastle County Court. Very rainy day, wet to the skin. Mother is extremely angry with me, never she had been worse before.

Fri 31st Settled all accounts with Mother. To Jones office but he was not at home. Mother is very indignant to me. Children all at home. Jenkin is very fast ruining them. Com Idt Ls with S't H but <u>Dge</u> <u>all</u> <u>Extlly</u>.

FEBRUARY 1862

Sat 1st David Thomas Shop Rhydowen[217] is from this day to pay all bills from Anne & Mary and also he is to receive their income from me by quarterly instalments. Appointed Mr Jones solicitor today to receive all rents from Tyssul Castle & to settle for me with Jenkin who has hitherto refused to pay main rents or to account for the money he received from me on account for the children. Both Jones and Thomas called at Tyssul Castle while Mother was there & she is now in a most terrible rage to me. Jenkin & the children are as well. This is one of the greatest storms that ever burst over my head as all my relations are fearful to me. Each and every one of them are ready to R le[218] me & all in consequence of my doing my duty & that in an upright, honest & straight-forward manner, so little do I care for them, every one.

Sun 2nd At home all the am. To Llanfair at pm with Sheraton. DK Br[219] at Dolgrogwys on my way home. Old Serv't A come here about 1 o'clock. She was very haughty & thinking herself very handsome. I never thought that she was so weak minded before and I never had so much of her as today, full of duplicity. I shall never want to see her again.

---

217. David Thomas, aged 48, single, shopkeeper and grocer. Lives with brother William, 35; sister Hannah, 30, housekeeper; Anne Jones, 34, housemaid. [*1861 Census, Llandyssil.*]
218. Rile? Rattle? It's not clear what he means.
219. Brandy.

Mon 3rd To Carmarthen with David to school to Swansea. Dk to elevation. Spent too much. Mr W. Thomas the haulier [?] of Mr L. [S?] Lewis[220] was buried today, saw corpse and the funeral. DK to elevation.

Tues 4th Unwell all the am from the effects of drinking Br yesterday. With E. Griffiths walking part of the pm, then relabeling fruit trees. Fine day. The cows of Ianto Bankyrhenbont[221] are impounded by Br Evan in the yard of the Porth since Saturday last.

Wednes 5th To Bwlchbychan to see Mr Pryse[222] but he was not at home. From there to Rhydyfyd-wydd. Quite a spring day, all kinds of birds have resumed their songs since the first day of the month. Mother has been to Tyssul Castle. Jenkin is all in all with her and I am the black of the black with her & no day is passed without her indulging her passions against me, but all on my back.

Thurs 6th To Dolgrogwys walking and enjoying each other's company, Griffiths and myself. Anne & Mary here. Had a letter today from Miss Evans Swansea stating that they have insisted upon Mr Titus Evans for a quarter's payment for the school for Anne & Mary & so he paid £12 for me & most likely without Miss Evans ever asking for them. I was terribly vexing for losing £12.

Fri 7th To Bwlchbychan soliciting Mr Pryse interest on behalf of John Gwarffynnon[223] for him to be put in the police force. Called at Llanfair. To the village at night, to Jones office & to Shop Jones & Amphlett, Mary & Anne went to school to Clifton today. To Jones office.

Sat 8th Alas Com Idt Ls with S't H last night. <u>Dge all Extlly</u>. The cattle of Evan Rees Bank Hen-bank are impounded in the Porth yard since this day week & one of the cows was sold on Monday to defray expenses covered for their keeping & tending them in there. Br Evan had given all the transactions about the cows from the beginning to Jones solicitor. Our cart sent to Carmarthen for the damaged Barley but failed to get any today.

Mon 10th Hard frost. Br Evan here for many hours at night, sober & apparently in trouble for impounding the cattle of his neighbour. They are (cattle) still at Porth Stile. Read all the Rules.

Tues 11th Gwlfair fair, fine day. At home till after supper when I went to Jones's office & from there to Shop Jones & with Jones again to Penbont, when we took a few glasses of Shrub. [?] There is a very bad report about Br Jenkin & A Ll- (Pencader), it is whispered all over the neighbourhood.[224]

Wednes 12th To Aberayron in the market cart with John James Wilks head buying damaged Linseed.[225] He & I bought 4 tons – one of which was for Jones Penrallt & one between Gelli farm & Dolgrogwys & two between Penbont & myself in equal shares. Drank some bitter beer.

220. Unable to identify these people.
221. See page 64, footnote 205.
222. John Pugh Vaughan Pryse (1818–1903).
223. John Jones, aged 20.
224. An intriguing reference to Rees's brother Jenkin.
225. John James, 39, farmer of 140 acres & inn keeper. [*1861 Census, Llanfihangel ar Arth.*]

Thurs 13th To Dolgrogwys all am about kiln drying the Linseed & walking & chatting with Griffiths. Sister here at pm. To the village & to Jones office at night.

Fri 14th At home all day till night, when I went over to Jones office but he was not at home. Lot of workmen here and all as lazy & idle as men can possibly be. Very fine day. My mind dwelling on the abuse of the 12 & om.

Sat 15th To Carmarthen. Very cold day. I was accompanied to & fro with Mr Rees Thomas Cribor. Jenkin was sued for amount for work by his Carpenter, who was building at Tyllyn. He paid yesterday & as the court was today. There is around a highly bad report of Idt Ls[226] taking place between him & A my niece. Com Idt with S't Hh this morning. <u>Dge</u> I <u>think all extlly</u>. She was out courting last night.

Mon 17th After the Foxhounds at Llanfair. Got drunk at Dolgrogwys on my way home.

After a further three days of intoxication . . .

Fri 21st Terribly poorly.

Sat 22nd Poorly. Spent – £2.10.0. Dr Davies attended yesterday & today & pronounced me in a dangerous state so far as my health goes. Suffered the most excritiating [sic] pain in my bowels occasioned, as Davies says, from congestion of the same together with my stomach. Sister here at pm. "O" what horrid pains I suffer mentally & corporally [sic] from the effects of drink.

Sun 23rd Horrid dreams all last night. No repose & no sound sleep. Got up rather early today. Reading and writing a new form for an oath today. Executed it by taking it on the New Testament in the presence of E. Griffiths Dolgrogwys at the lower end of Ynys Llanfair on the side of Dolgrogwys by & under an oak tree. Fine & warm day but fearful gloomy & despondent to me. If I should vault [?] this oath God knows what must speedily come of me as I now only escaped from a Drunkard's & premature grave.

Mon 24th Began a reformed life. Read R & everything. I am determined to continue it in future & then what a happy being should I be. Many workmen here.

Tues 25th Mother most angry with me continually & by this time there is no doubt that there is a deep state of enmity in her heart against me. Johnny was sent from home by her & Jenkin owning to his having three large pimples on his neck. Owing to M scolding me most terrific this evening that I could not Sleep by myself so Com Idt Ls with H. Dge <u>all extelly</u>.

---

226. That changeable code for sex.

Wednes 26th To Dolgrogwys at am having a little chat with Evan. Wind high from the East & freezing at night. The Brynog Fox hounds started a fox from Vronfynnonbwla & after going round this land he made for Llanfair & towards Pantydefaid & from there again I dare say. Fine day.

Thurs 27th To Llanfair at pm. Had a long conversation with Capt Sheraton. John Rees Penalltgerdyn lad married today. Suffering from Rheumatism very badly in my left arm, especially my wrist.

Fri 28th Out with the working men all day. High & cold wind blowing from the East for the last 5 days. Making new railings in the meadow. Post was tarred made of the heart of Larch from Alltyglyn. Br Evan sent two brace plovers here, the first of the Kind ever was to my hand. February has expired & it proved a most Deplorable month for me owing to drinking, among other things. I have not for a minute enjoyed the finer feelings of nature this month. Trusting that the next will be better.

MARCH 1862

Sat 1st To Carmarthen. Kept my pledge but unfortunately after coming home, Com Idt Ls with S't H. <u>Dge all xtlly</u>.

Mon 3rd There is three inches snow. E. Griffiths & myself followed the foot prints of a fox to his lair above Ffynnonbwla where I shot at him and wounded him but he went away again & we followed him for some distance. Snowing now & then all day.

Thurs 6th Many person came here to settle. To a vestry at Llanfihangel, tasting not a drop. Terrible rainy this afternoon & yesterday. Com Idt Ls with S't H. Dge all extlly.

Fri 7th To Llandyssil & there got DK. Slept at the Druggist for stay all night. Went home about 5am.

Sat 8th Awful unwell, all day in bed.

Sun 9th In bed most of the day very unwell. Got DK, this time on resin wine alone.

Tues 11th Very unwell & no sleep at night. Bad cold, cough with shortness of breath, all bad symptoms of long life.

Wednes 12th To Carmarthen receiving interest for Llangunllo & redeeming their plate from the Jeweller.

Mon 17th To Court farm. Alas Com Idt Ls with S't Hh. Dge <u>all extlly</u>. Not well, cough & cold still.

Wednes 19th Marking Fir for cutting all am. To Ffynnonbwla at the pm & fishing from there down but no rise. High wind from the East & very cold. To Jones office last night but he was not at home. Br David is more quiet today. He has been for the last fortnight very restless & ill tempered. M is still very indignant to me & pitying Jenkin very much. He is about to be served with a notice to quit to see if he will pay the rents due.

Thurs 20th At home all day. Settling with the masons, very lazy & stupid & sleepy. Com Idt Ls with S't H. Dge <u>all extlly</u>.

Fri 21st The earth once more this year is covered with snow three inches thick, but soon melted. Out with the gun taking Fox, E. Griffiths & David Ffynnonbwla with me.

Sat 22nd Mr Jones Solit'r served Mr J. Thomas Tyssul Castle with notice to quit on account of his refusing to pay any rent since & before the death of the testator. The interest of the arrears amounts to £7.5.0 for which I am responsible & must pay. Jenkin after receiving the notice became very excited & indulgent in his evil passions so terrific as to charge me with every kind of wickedness, viz dishonesty, and theft. Jones came over here to tell me of everything. If he will neither pay nor give a note for the amount Jones is to get a distress upon his goods within 14 days. He sent for Mother to meet him at the lodge at dusk but I do not know what passed between them. Jenkin's principles have become very bad of late & most likely if not a speedy change will take place his future looks very gloomy & miserable for him.[227]

Mon 24th S't H informed me this morning that she was enfille.[228] It took so much effect that I got drunk at Cifing cottage.[229] Slept there that night.

Three days of intoxication until . . .

Fri 28th Quite out of my senses.

Sat 29th Farewell to this world.

Sun 30th D D S about S't H.[230] Indescribable mental anguish accompanied with awful pain. I have taken some medicine today though I have no hope or wish to ever to get well again. O God have mercy upon me & take me away from this world which I have made too miserable for myself to live in any more.

Mon 31st The senses of seeing and hearing have greatly impaired. Miserable beyond description. No appetite & hardly no life in me, but I feel as if I was on the brink of the grave, which would be a paradise to me now & for ever again.

227. Rees here serves his brother Jenkin with a notice to quit for nonpayment of rent.
228. Hannah is pregnant.
229. This place name is nearly illegible in the diary.
230. The diarist consults Dr Davies for advice about terminating Hannah's pregnancy.

GLOOMY APRIL 1862

Tues 1st At home all day, no writing or reading but labouring under the most terrific mental anguish. It would now certainly be a great relief to me if I knew that I would have only a few days to live. S't Hannah had begun the ft [st?] B.le from DD to get rid of the ch-d.[231]

Wednes 2nd Fishing with worm with Dio Ffynnonbwla all day. River too large, overflowing its Banks. Awful low spirits all day.

Thurs 3rd At home all day in a half dead state owing to what exists which undoubtedly will send me into premature Grave. Very wet weather.

Fri 4th Writing at am. With Mr Amphlett at pm cutting pea sticks. Lovely day to be out but gloomy on me wherever I go with no hope of its ever getting better owing to S't H. I do not really think that I shall be able to read anything again.

Sat 5th Despairing all day. Sleepy all am. No taste for anything, either reading or writing. M is going every other night to meet Jenkin by Tanrallt Lodge. She has great enmity towards me which will not likely decrease again. To DD[232] last night about H. To Dolgrogwys and Ffynnonbwla at am. To Mr Jones office relative to the dispute between Jenkin & myself. My present cause of vexation has more or less affected my head.

Sun 6th Chapel at am. Mr Rees Thomas here at pm, also Mr David Thomas Rhydowen about Anne & Mary's affairs. No man nor minister has ever been so much busy as I am with Jenkin. M is as bitter against me as possible. I am not now again going to her house as she turns her head from me when I go in.

Mon 7th To New Inn,[233] bought a Bee hive today. Drank some Beer at New Inn. Calls at Wilkes head. Heard there that Jenkin is abusing me most shamefully. I am a liar drunkard, swindler & awfully of bad principle in every way whatever. To the village at night for medicine for S't H from DD. Com Idt Ls with her D-v-l. Dge all extlly.

Tues 8th With Amphlett up to where the Clettwr falls into the Tivy & tried fishing from there down as far as Penalltgerdyn. Captured myself about 2 dozen. Went very despondent before reached home. The fir all almost in full foliage now & the blossoms of the plums are open & those of the cherry partially. Fine day but gloomy upon me. To Jones office at night.

Thurs 10th Ffair blodau day. Been over myself to meet Mr Evans Court, who came down at the special request of Jenkin to make up between us about the accounts. I refused to leave it to be

---

231. I assume this to be *"Servant Hannah has begun the first bottle from Dr Davies to get rid of the child."*
232. Dr Davies.
233. New Inn, Rhydowen.

decided to arbitration owing that it was not my own money but that of little Jane. Very fine day. Rev'd T. Thomas here since last night.

Fri 11th To Newcastle Emlyn. To the sale of Blaendyffryn farms which Mr Lloyd Davies[234] bought of Lloyd Glansefin.[235] I intended myself to buy Tavarn farm adjoining Rhydyfine[236] for Johnny but it went for £895, much too high. Dk to elevation. Com Idt with S't H. Dge all extlly.

Sun 13th Reading at am, chapel at pm but the pangs of a guilty conscience was so great that I could not show my face with them so it was better for me to remain at home till my present trouble will be over.

Mon 14th Mr Rees Thomas auctioneer at pm. To Jones office at am respecting the agreement of Cwmnant. Had the third B-ll [bottle] with Dr D last Saturday night for S't H.[237] Rainy.

Tues 15th To Carmarthen. Unwell from a bad cold.

Wednes 16th S't H in a bad temper & threatened me about the future most awfully last night. Got into such a despondency from that time that I could not know what I was doing. Took no victuals of any kind of food since at Carmarthen yesterday. Com Idt Ls with her D – l this morning. <u>Dge all extlly</u>. She came bad to me then. "O" how I am under her devilish feet. Really I wish my life was at an end as I am gone too far in despondency to be of any service to myself or anyone else in future. Took no food all day but labouring under great despondency & very bitterly at time.

Thurs 17th Almost quite blind & very weak & despondent. Br David was raving mad yesterday & last night. If he caught hold of me last night undoubtedly he would have relieved me from my present miserable state in a few minutes but I hid myself from his sight as he was dreadful worse than I ever saw him before. Br Evan was here & he was just as mad as David. David Llanfair came home for the holidays from Swansea school. Sent a cart to meet him to Conwil station.

Fri 18th Dr D been here examining S't Hh & thought that she is not pregnant, consequently I was in ecstasy. Though still he may not be certain yet however I have hope once more. The last Menstruation took place 15th of last February. Dr D came first to examine her Sun 30 March.

Sat 19th David Llanfair has been to Court farm from yesterday but his Grand papa was not at home. When he (David) came home here he was very proud and haughty. He told me when going to bed that he wanted very much to see his Grandfather & Mr Jones Llwyngroes.[238] I asked for what purpose he wished to see Mr Jones he replied "O" That belongs to me, & again he said he should go to spend the holidays at Llaethlliw in future. His tone was very defiant to me & he often repeated these words, "I don't care for anything," or "What do I care for anyone." The poor fellow

234. John Lloyd Davies of Alltrodyn.
235. Edward Pryce Lloyd (1786–1868) of Glansefin, Llangadog.
236. I have been unable to trace these properties. They are evidently farms on the Blaendyffryn estate.
237. Still trying to effect an abortion.
238. William Jones of Llwynygroes, Llanwnnen. [Francis Jones, *Historic Cardiganshire Homes & Their Families*.]

is going fast in the wrong way. There are very many sense that no good will become of him, though his evil disposition must be almost all attributed to Jenkin, who was taking him every night mostly with him to drink while he, David, was there during the holidays.

Sun 20th At home all day. Easter Sunday. People generally wore some new dress today. Weather very wet.

Wed 23rd To NC Emlyn. Br Evan's trial for impounding the cattle of Evan Rees Bankyrhenbont took place. My brother lost it on every step. When my brother was examined he was too bold & every word he said was injurious to his own side & his witnesses' testimony were also injurious to their own side. Asked David whether he would remain at Swansea school after this quarter which ends at Midsummer. He said that he would not & then he began taking me up, hinting that I am as an executor pocketing his money and that "he is now ready to meet for me & that his uncle Llaethlliw will come upon me." Then he left for Tyssil Castle. I shall never forget his words. This is the payment I receive for all my time, trouble & expense relative to Llanfair's affairs.

Thurs 24th Com Idt Ls with S't Hh this morning in a chair. <u>Dge all extlly</u> certain. Rev'd T. Evans here after the accounts. Rainy all day. David left for school with Jenkin this morning.

Sat 26th About my accounts from seven in the morning till 12 at night. He leaves about 5 o'clock & neither my brother David's account nor those of Llanfair are now in a more forward state than when he came here. My head has become quite giddy today so am unable to do anything whatever. O what trouble I get & how miserable I am.

Mon 28th Very sleepy & despondent all the am, however was very active all pm going over my accounts. Today is the warmest and most lovely day we have had this year. Heard the corncrake last Thursday & the cuckoo yesterday in Vron Yet Wen. All the cherry, plum & pears are past their full bloom. The trees (cherries) looked beautifully in the meadow last week, the blossoms in clusters & with no leaves.

Wednes 30th Auction of the letting of land at Llanfair. Fine day. Com Idt with S't Hh. Dge <u>all Extlly</u> & am quite certain too.

GLOOMY MAY 1862

Thurs 1st Awful despondency in consequence of S't Hh. Drank a good deal all day but too low Spirited to get Dk. Dr D here examined H & said that she is pregnant.

Sat 3rd Awful Despondent still. Weather warm & fine but alas dark to me. I really believe that my head is very much affected in consequence of my present trouble & not knowing what will be the result either of the cause of my trouble or its effect upon myself.

Sun 4th At home until afternoon when I went by Ffynnonbwla & Dolgrogwys. Fine day, the high winds of previous days being calmed. The trees (Beech & few others) have extended their leaves to about half their full size. M was at Tyssil Castle all yesterday & today, she shows her enmity towards me in a feverish manner. Never have I been before in such a state as i am now since the 24 of last March.[239]

Wednes 7th Out with the workmen all day beginning sowing mangles. O what a difficult job to keep the Devilish Hh pleased. I am completely at a lost like a mouse at the mercy of the cat. Not for a minute happy.

Thurs 8th Unwell from the effects of last night's debauch. Drank to half drunk at the Druggist shop. Dio Ffynnonbwla, Watty & S't Evan were also part DK, the two former with Br Evan at the Union Club & the latter partly with me. I cannot help myself at present as my Grief is almost unsupportable owing entirely to S't H, with whom <u>Com Idt Ls</u>. Dge <u>I think all extlly</u>.

Fri 9th Dr D was here to see little Jane. He pronounced H to be pregnant & the medicine was discontinued. I got into such mental trouble as to get Dk. Idt Ls with S't H. Dge on purpose this time all <u>intlly</u>.

A four day binge follows until:

Wednes 14th Mad of mental anguish.

Fri 16th Out with the workmen finishing stripping oak. 1—1 om.

Sat 17th At Carmarthen. On my way home my Spirits were getting more low as I was nearing home owing to the state of S't H, who began to attack me as soon as I entered the house.

Sun 18th To chapel at am. To Dolgrogwys & Ffynnonbwla at pm and there I was till sunset. I truly find the effects of my present trouble strong in my mind, which is no little impairment & God only knows how I shall be in six months hence. No enjoyment for me again I am afraid or at least have only a faint hope. Fine weather still & warm today.

A six-day binge begins on Thursday May 22. He sleeps with Hannah on Tuesday 27th and on Wednes 28th he reports: Wild with madness & very ill.

Thurs 29th At Llanfair at am. Out with the workmen all pm. Had not a moment's repose last night but in a drowsy state part of the time & when in that state I was seeing & talking to my brothers Thomas & John believing that they were by my bedside advising me not to get in that state again. They were apparently, poor brothers, speaking in the lowest manner.[240]

Fri 30th Got up from bed this morning between 1 & 2 to see about the Gutters owing to a most awful shower of rain at the time & really I never saw such a shower in my life before. Had I been

---

239. When Hannah told him she was pregnant.
240. These are his dead elder brothers.

asleep that night & not hearing the rain my loss would be heavy as the water would rush into the house, as the space between Mother's house & that of my own was like a pond owing to the gutter being stopped with water, and the pigs would have drowned in the pig sty. There was no lightning nor thunder at the time. The shower abated before 2am. Went to the funeral of the daughter of David Charles Coedfoel.[241] To Llanfair fishing with worms with Capt Sh all pm.

Sat 31st Out with the workmen & to Llanfair at pm. Lovely day & warm. So ended May, the most troublesome upon me. Never have I experienced such a month before & never will a worse one in every way.

JUNE 1862

Mon 2nd Many workmen here. Whitewashed the house today. Sister here, gave her an old cheese as a present. Alas Com Idt Ls with the devil S't H in the chair. Dge all extlly.

Tues 3rd To Ffair Newydd Carmarthen. Saw Heenan the prize fighter in a circus.[242] Conducted myself with the utmost propriety & spent only what was reasonable. Very warm day.

Wednes 4th The procession day of the UBC.[243] At home myself all day, many strangers here. Dr D examined S't Hh & found her to be so pregnant.

Sun 8th Com Idt Ls with S't Hh tonight. Dge all internally, consequently was in a most deplorable mental anguish all day. Never I think I have been in such a state before. Dk some spirits but was low Spirited for it to take any effect whatever. Mr R. Thomas Cribor here to dinner.

Mon 9th Late in bed, much despondency still. However was out with the workmen all day & a beautiful day it was. O how happy I should be if my present cause of trouble would be over.

Wednes 11th Sul gwyn fair at Lampeter to sell the mare of Llangunllo. Awful rainy too.

Thurs 12th Memorable night on account of Dr Davies had been here about 12pm to pursue abortion on S't H.

Fri 13th S't H same as usual yet. My anxiety as to the future is indescribable as to the effect.

Sat 14th To Carmarthen. The children of Llanfair came home from school today & no doubt none of them will come here. Fine day.

---

241. David Charles, Coedfoel: farmer's son David Charles, aged 36, lives with his mother Catherine, a widow of 62 and two unmarried sisters on a farm of 87 acres. His daughter must live with her (un-named) mother. [*1861 Census, Llandyssil.*]
242. John Carmel Heenan (1833–1873), the American bare knuckle fighter known as "The Bernici Boy", famous for slugging it out for 37 rounds with legendary Brighton prize-fighter Tom Sayers in one of the last great bare knuckle fights at Farnborough, Hampshire, on April 17, 1860. After two hours and 20 minutes, Heenan's corner jumped in to stop the fight, which was then declared a draw. This bloody fight between two famous prize fighters helped to put an end to bare fist fighting in Britain.
243. Union Benefit Club.

Mon 16th Very warm day. To Llanfair about making some plan for having net fishing salmon as usual. Capt Sheraton is terribly against the coracles.

Tues 17th At home all am, sleepy. Fishing for salmon with Amphlett at pm, had seen none. Very rainy. Jenkin is as desperate to me as any man can be to the other.

Wednes 18th To Newcastle Emlyn to hear the trials at the County Court. Received a good deal of instruction therein. To Ebenezer[244] at 6 to hear two sermons by Independent preachers.

Thurs 19th Dr D here late night re-examining S't H & then gave her a Strong dose. Today she is confined in bed very ill. Mother sent for Dr D to see S't Hh at am today and gave some physic to her. She in bed all day. Awful fear & anxiety as to the result. Never I have been in so much trouble. Br Evan here all last night till breakfast this morning. Many persons attended to have their seed hay in today but heavy rain hit quite unexpectedly.

Fri 20th To the Drugs Shop this morning. Terrible fear & awful mental anxiety as to the result of H. Not able to read nor write. Cold day. Very despondent. Sister here at pm. Smoking fearfully.

The diarist takes refuge again in binge drinking from Saturday 21st to Wednesday 25th.

Thurs 26th Bewildered (mowing hay).

Fri 27th Out making hay, weather thundery. I felt myself once more convalescent. Capt Sheraton is getting a part of his hay in.

Sat 28th Making hay all day, about 20 with it. Fine day, high wind.

Sun 29th At home all day, over Farm and part of Dolgrogwys for a walk at pm, Dio Ffynnonbwla & Watty also. We met David Rees Sailor & David & Johnny at Lodge & we all went together as far as Galltyetwen, when the two former entered the plantation & sneaked away somewhere & never returned to us any more, though we stayed there for about an hour. Johnny sneaked & slipped back at Lodge. Rainy in the evening.

Mon 30th Making hay and having it in & in good condition. Sent over to the village after dinner to have the assistance of those whom I declined in the morning owing that I thought the hay would not be in a fit state to be ricked. About 40 persons or more tendered their assistance so we were in all about between 60 & 70 persons. Capt Sheraton came over & remained full two hours.

JULY 1862

Tues 1st To Llanfair at am, had a long chat with Capt Sh. I feel very tired since yesterday.

---

244. Ebenezer Independent Chapel, Newcastle Emlyn.

Wednes 2nd Dr D Examined S't H. Mother was at Tyssil Castle and she came home full of enmity towards me & gave utterance now & then to her rage against me. She is since last March suppressing her temper as much as possible. Johnny & Grace Llangunllo came here for to stay a few days. I am wild from fear and remorse on account of S't H. O how happy should I be once more should I get over my present trouble.

Sat 5th Int[oxicated]. Dr D here about H, but failed.

The following Sunday, Monday, Tuesday and Wednesday are again spent bingeing alcohol. On Thursday, 4th, Dr Davies is called out to treat the diarist.

Fri 11th Bewildered & very unwell.

Sat 12th No repose all last night & quite in bewildered state still, yes in a state I have never been in before owing entirely to H.

Fri 18th At Llanfair all day assisting Capt Sh to have the hay in. Dined at 2 o'clock there. Young Longcroft Llanina[245] was also there. Dk to half drunk just before leaving.

Sat 19th Out all day & in terrible Mental anguish in consequence of the state of S't H. I am truly in a most miserable condition. I wish I was to die now.

Tues 22nd Rainy. Nothing but reading some papers. To Dolgrogwys at pm. They were mowing. Still in awful anxiety & fear, no mental ease. Great numbers about here are mowing today.

Thurs 24th Rainy at am. Anne Llanfair has been here being now the 5th time & she never came to call on me and I have not had an opportunity to speak to her yet. She & her brother David & her sister there are telling hard lies upon me all over the County & David is threatening me most terribly & as he says that he ruin me as soon as his uncle Llaethlliw will come home. The weather has & still continues very unfavourable for the hay harvest. Rain more or less every day for the last seven weeks of more. All the hay about here is now cut.

Fri 25th Beautiful fine day. Farm, Vrongoch & Blaenwaun had their hay in today. The Farm's hay was much too fresh & consequently will heat in the stack too much. Anne Llanfair here all day but she came not to me.

Sat 26th At Dolgrogwys all am, at Nantegryd all pm. Both were having their hay in & in good condition. Mother asked me to let Tyssil Castle to her in order for her to let it to Jenkin. My reply to her was that as long as Jenkin was advising the children to refuse everything I ask of them he should never have it on any account whatever, therefore Mother became very indignant to me. Offered the place to her if Evan would leave Nantegryd & come to live there.

---

245. A son of Charles Richard Longcroft, of Llanina near New Quay – possibly Charles Edward Longcroft.

Mon 28th At Llanfair mowing our hay. There without taking any food from 7am till 5pm. Very hot night. 2—2 unavoidably.[246]

The next two days are spent making hay at Llanfair.

Thurs 31st At Llanfair turning the course of the river at Ynysygu. Lot of workmen there, rainy all day.

AUGUST 1862

Fri 1st Signed and swore before E. G. Dolgrogwys that I would abstain from all intoxicating drink from this day to the end of the present year. Paid S't Hh towards the maintenance of her Child for one year ending November 1863, paid in all £7/5/0. From this day I am resolved to lead a better life, yea quite a religious & moral life.

Sat 2nd Not well, cough & rheum. Mr & Mrs Jones Gellifaharan called & it seems that he now intends practising here private. He will get a good practice.

Sun 3rd At home all am, for a walk with Dio Carpt & Watty over Llanfair. Sat a long time in Pentybach. Killed a pretty large adder there. Fine & warm day. Not well myself.

Tues 5th To Court farm at the request of the old Gentleman to defend myself against the complaints of David Llanfair, who unjustly accused me for not giving any money to him to go to school. He was there the day before, and what heaps of falsehoods. Said again my bit to no avail. Awful showers, wet to the skin in going & coming.

Wednes 6th To Llanfair to see about the river. Anne came here to ask for pocket money for her Br David, who said that he will never come to ask for any money from me himself. Anne's language was haughty & defiant, though I apparently took no notice of it. Mother is at Carmarthen since last Monday repairing Waundu.[247]

Thurs 7th I was working in the river all day till 4 o'clock driving a large accumulation of sand away by the heavy water from Ynisygru Llanfair as the river was wearing the bank away seriously on the side. My hands got all blistered & more tired from working than I ever have been before. Dr Davies & Jenkin paid me a visit in the evening. The children left for school to Bristol.

Fri 8th The children of Llanfair left Carmarthen for school today. David indulged his bad passions to the utmost extent by threatening me with a lawsuit for turning a little of the course of the river at Ynysugri, thereby saving his island on this side from being carried away as is daily the case at

---

246. Another example of a variable code that Rees uses at the end of each entry in his diary. I have usually edited this out as there is no way of saying what it indicates.
247. Also written as Waundew.

present, more or less. David Llangunllo came here to ask for money (loan) of £20. Had none to leave him.

Sun 10th With Evan Dolgrogwys walking by the river side, rather cold day. Preparing myself for going to Carmarthen tomorrow in order to leave for London by the excursion train on Tuesday.

Mon 11th Left here in my cart for Carmarthen, there to go by next morning excursion train to London. Slept at Carmarthen tonight. Mother was there with my workmen repairing Waundew since last Tuesday, also little Jane with her. Spent a good sum.

Tues 12th Left by the 8 o'clock excursion train for London. Was there about 8pm. Took a lodgings with Morris at Falcon Tavern, Falcon Square.

Wednes 13th Called at Mrs William Bevis Mark. S't Mary are for Miss Jane Jones Nantremenyn[248] & Miss Jeremy[249] who came up by the same train with me but not in the same carriage. Took them to see the exhibition, to see that we went up.[250] Jenkin & the children of Llanfair, all but Jane, saw me it seems then also I saw them but did not go to them, nor they neither came to me.

Thurs 14th To the Exhibition by myself today, also to the adjoining grounds called Kensington Gardens. Miss Jones & Miss Jeremy were there accompanied with Mr Jeremy. Met many Welsh friends at Mr Williams at night & there Dk to elevation.

Fri 15th Called on Misses Jones & Jeremy at noon & took them to the British Museum & Madam Tussauds. They were both awfully tired & the former could hardly walk, though we engaged a cab in going & coming.

Sat 16th Took a boat by myself at London Bridge to Westminster. Visited the Houses of Parliament, Covent Garden Market, National Gallery & took a lounge through St James's Park & St Paul's. Weather rainy. Miss Jones and Jeremy at home.

Sun 17th With David Beeham Court by boat up to Kew Gardens. All over the gardens, though it was rainy all day. Large lumps like those of Bull or Farcy on horses all over my body, accompanied with itching & consequently very uncomfortable & leaving for home. Miss Jones and Jeremy all day at home.

Mon 18th Up early this morning to see Billingsgate Market. There were heaps of salmon there. Then lounged in the principle streets. Evans Pistill, David Evans Union & his brother Thomas came up & look lodgings with Morris. They were all half Dk.

248. Jane Jones is a 43-year-old unmarried laundress who has a house servant called Mary Davies, aged 32. The house is written in the 1861 census as Nantyrymenyn.
249. Not known.
250. The International Exhibition, Kensington Gardens, 1862.

Tues 19th Went by train to Sydenham Place being the Foustard [?] feast day there. Saw Blondin walking up a rope 60ft high.[251] Found the Llandysilians, just went in with them all. There were about 83,000 visitors present.

Wednes 20th Evans Pistill[252] & myself called upon Miss Jones & Jeremy & went by boat to Westminster Bridge, visited the Houses of Parliament, Westminster Abbey, round St James's Park, up Constitution Hill & lastly to the Exhibition. Evans & myself walked home from there & we both got very tired. David Evans was half Dk.

Thurs 21st With Evans Pistill & Thomas Union[253] & Davis Peakin[254] went to the Exhibition. To Dr Hann's Museum Eldorado where females were dancing almost quite naked & where was plenty of drink.

Fri 22nd With Miss Jones & Jeremy to the Crystal Palace. We saw Blondin dancing upon a low rope. David Evans at the square Dk. Evans Pistill was scandalous, penniless, shameful to the extreme.

Sat 23rd Evans Pistill & myself with Miss Jones & Jeremy to the Tower & Thames tunnel & that was all my lounge in London.

Sun 24th William Thomas Union & myself went by boat to Greenwich Park & there spent the last day in London. Thomas was behaving like a Gentleman in all respects. David Evans was half drunk every evening he was there till Friday. From that day out he was quite drunk from morning to evening and would have been once taken to the lock-up house had M & William not interfered & took him home to the lodgings. Evans Pistill acted in a most mean & low manner. He would take from the hands of everyone plenty of drink & but would never pay a penny himself. He preferred staying at his lodgings then to go out for fear that he should have to spend some money. He never paid his share at any place, in truth his perniciousness amounted to perfect dishonesty. No more of his company.[255]

Mon 25th Thomas Union & David Evans, Evans Pistill & myself left Paddington Station at ¼ to 8 this morning & arrived at Carmarthen at ½ past 8pm. All of us left Carmarthen again for our relative homes, arrived about one very tired. I spent, including for a new hat & everything, £12/8/10. Mother gave me gratuitously on my leaving Carmarthen for London the sum of £1.

---

251. French daredevil acrobat Charles Blondin (1824–1897) became famous as the first person to walk across Niagara Falls on a tightrope. In 1862 Blondin earned £1,200 for 12 performances at the Crystal Palace in Sydenham, a huge sum of money at that time. He walked on a tightrope at a height of 180ft, pushing his five-year-old daughter Adele in a wheelbarrow. The press and public were horrified and the Home Secretary ordered him to stop putting the child at risk. During subsequent performances he performed his regular repertoire, including cooking an omelet on the high wire, turning somersaults and walking on stilts, all of which were sufficiently dangerous and breathtaking to satisfy the huge crowds. His appearances caused Charles Dickens to remark: "Half of London is here eager for some dreadful accident."
252. David Evans of Pistill Storehouse in Llandysul.
253. This is one of several people called William Thomas living in Llandysul. He is not listed in the census at the Union Tavern and may be an official of the Union Benefit Fund.
254. Unknown.
255. But see the following day.

Tues 26th Got up early at home this morning, though very tired, & walked about a good deal. Corn was ripe & we shall begin cutting tomorrow.

Thurs 28th Rent audit of Llanfair. They paid pretty well. Davis Cwmmanty[256] is it seems going stupid to leave & had already been with Mitchell to have his advice. David nephew has been advised not to leave his farm & telling him that I had no authority to eject. O what a wicked child, not yet 16. His threats to me are desperate in the extreme, his last threats were owing that I was changing the course of the river at Dolecwmisha to prevent it from making further encroachment on Llanfair island on this side & also on Dolgrogwys side. He was the last time he was at home in an open enmity to me & was incited with Jenkin to the highest pitch. He is now in school in Bristol in the same town as his sisters are. No good will likely come of him as he will never be brought down to work. He is awfully & fearfully doing underhand work. There is very great duplicity about him. In a word he is a thorough wicked fellow.

There are three minor entries detailing paperwork and inconsequential matters before the diary runs out of pages.

---

256. Possibly Enoch Davies, aged 20, employed as a carter at Cwmandwy. [*1861 Census, Llandyssil.*]

Appendix 1

A CHILD'S DIARY. DAVID THOMAS (1846–1882)
[transcribed exactly in sequence and as written in a small black notebook]
Ref: Pembrokeshire Record Office D/Wil/227.

Friday November 20th 1863 We came down to Carmarthen to live. We started from Tyssul Castle between two & three in the afternoon and slept at our lodgings that night.

Acct of what things I got from Uncle Jenkin.

Novbr 20th I bought a lump of scented soap from him at our lodgings, paid 3.

Nov 21st Lent me 3 pences.

Dec 18th Lent me one shilling. He also lent me two shillings a time before that. That was the 16th 1863.

What Bills to pay, Novbr 20th. Paid T. E. Jones, general merchant, for one bushel of oats purchased July 2 3/3 & one bushel of bran purchased Aug 1 for Charley[1] 1/3. Total 4/6.

Saturday December 5th, 1863
Uncle Rees came down to town. I did not see him but he left a sovereign with Mr Titus Evans for me, which I had given on Saturday evening when I went there with uncle Jenkin.

My bill that uncle Rees paid to Dr Davies . . . Bill of Purchase total 13/6
Cerate & lint 1/- visit 2/6
Ointment & lint 1/6d visit 2/6; visit 2/6; mixture 2/6; cerate lint & plaster 1

The last bill that uncle Rees paid for Johnny for Doctor Davies
visit 2/6; powder 1; linement (x2) 1/6 = total 6/6

Account of what things to buy from Nov 20th
Oct 21st bought a ledger 1/-
Oct 21st Bought a small account book 6d
Oct 21st Bought a neck tie 1/-
Oct 21st Bought a weekly illustrated London News 1d

---

1. His uncle's pony.

84

Oct 20th Uncle Jenkin gave me half a crown to buy some socks for Johnny.[2] I bought four pair at sixpence each but they would not fit him and they were sent back. He tried many other pairs but could not get any to fit him.

Monday Nov 23rd 1863 I lent my mare to Mrs Thomas Maesycrigie Arms, Carmarthen to go to Abergwily to bury her sister. She sent her sister down to our lodgings on Monday morning to ask me to lend her the mare. On Friday Nov 20th 1863 Uncle Evan Nantegryd gave me Vic, a little bitch that was kept at Graig Nantegryd. He came down with me to Tyssul Castle that morning. He lent me his mare after dinner to go up and fetch the little bitch and as I was bringing her back I met Uncle Evan near Penpwll. He was very savage and told me to get off his horse and to let the little bitch go. I did so directly.

Dec 19th I went up to Mr Parry the engine house. Rowe came in after me. We sat down there talking till about seven o'clock until after nine o'clock in the evening. We then all three of us went out together for a walk. We went up as far as Picton and back again as far as the Parade. Rowe and Perry then came with me as far as the door of our lodgings. I then wished them good night and I went up stairs. When I got up there Uncle Jenkin was alone and at supper. I went into him, I should say he had been drinking. He immediately began scolding me and said that I must not have my own way but that I must obey him and not stay out so late or I was to leave him immediately. I walked straight up to bed. After next morning he was allright, so that ended.

Dec 19th[3] Mr Griffiths my head master at Bedland[4] called upon us and we went up and down and showed it to him altogether. He went off down to Milford Saturday night and came back Sunday morning and was at Carmarthen between twelve & one o'clock middle day on Sunday to take dinner with us and then we had a gig from the Boar's Head hotel which Uncle paid nine shillings for. I and Mr Griffiths went together in this gig up to Llanfair. We went all over the house and into the farm yard and then we drove home to Carmarthen through Llandyssil and Griffiths slept Sunday night at the Ivy Bush. He said he would come down to us for breakfast if he did not over sleep himself. He did not come down and we did not see him after Sunday night.

Dec 30th I rode Charley, Uncle Jenkin's pony, up to Llanfair. I left the pony at Llanfair & took my little pony across the river to Dôl-llan. As I was going into the house I met Grandmama by her outer kitchen. I then went to Uncle Rees house. I knocked at the door. He opened the door himself. I then went down with him to his study. The first thing he did was to read the letter that Miss Evans Llaethlliw had written to him informing him of Uncle Evan's death and asking him to go to the funeral. Just as he finished reading the letter M. Davies Llangunllo came in. We went down to the parlour & had some bread & cheese & beer and as I was leaving Uncle Rees came with me into the station and gave me four pence to pay the expense up to funeral from Carmarthen. I then went from him to Grandmama's house. She gave me two glasses of whisky, some bread & butter & biscuits & a pear & a shilling. I then went from there to Llanfair & sent Dio with Uncle's pony up

2. His brother.
3. December 19th again.
4. I've been unable to place this school.

to Pencader & I rode my own pony up to Nantegryd. I stayed there for a short time and I then went from there to Pencader & changed pony & then went back to Carmarthen and that day finished like that.

He specifies that Uncle Evan returned home & then returned again to Llandyssil for the purpose of procuring the payment of the balance of 25,000. As soon as Uncle Evan had had the mortgage granted he returned to Llaethlliw and one day my sister Mary & my brother Johnny & myself went up to Llaethlliw. Uncle Evan & grandfather were busily writing orders for the creditors for them to get the money at the bank Aberayron. Uncle Evan sent a man that day to Dôl-llan with a letter asking my Uncle Rees if he would come up the following day. We slept there that night. Uncle Rees came up on the following day. Uncle Evan & Uncle Rees had a private conversation. I went in to the parlour where they were and stayed there with them and I heard Uncle Evan repeatedly asking my Uncle Rees to write a short time for the money and at the same time Uncle Evan was forcing drink upon my Uncle Rees. He did drink rather hard and before he went from them he got very drunk. When he was going to start home he returned twice to the house for yet some more drink which he got and I have heard my Uncle Rees say himself that he was drunk that day. He told me that as he was going through Llandyssil he asked Thomas Lias the blacksmith if he was going the right way to which he had passed a long way before he had come to Llandyssil and Uncle Rees specifies in his affidavit that he could not find Uncle Evan address in Llandyssil.

Uncle Rees sent for me to meet him one night either at the latter end of December 1862 or at the beginning of January 1863 and he told me that he should very much like to find out Uncle Evan's address in Llandyssil and asked me if I would go up to Court Farm on the following day to try to get Grandfather to help me. I went off to Court Farm on the following day and Grandpapa told me his address. I took it to my Uncle Rees that night and to show that the address was not a false one I sent a letter from my Uncle Evan by that address and he sent me an answer which I received on 29th January 1863 which letter I have now in my possession.

Appendix 2

DÔL-LLAN – THE HISTORY OF THE HOUSE
[much of this appendix relies on two articles by Thomas Lloyd
in the Friends of Hafod Newsletter, Numbers 11 and 12].

Dôl-llan is an old foundation, dating back certainly to the 16th century and probably before, and in its present form may have been touched by the distinctive hand of the famous Regency architect John Nash. That conjecture is open to debate as there appears to be no written reference. What is beyond doubt is that it was home at one time to the late 18th century agricultural improver Dr David Stevenson of Doctors' Commons, who extended what was no more than a plain two storey farmhouse and built a modern farmhouse and quadrangle of outbuildings at Dôl-llan Ucha, now known as Farmyard. And this work was carried out at a time when Nash was active in Wales, and engaged by one of Stevenson's closest friends in Wales – Thomas Johnes of Hafod.

One of the earliest references to Dôl-llan is a quit claim in Latin dated 22 July 1546 by which John ap Howell ap Rhydderch and William ap John ap Howell (his son) of Carmarthen and Griffith ap John Thomas of Llanpumpsaint conveyed *Tire dole y llay* to Dafydd ap Dafydd of Glfachwen near Llandysul.[1] Dafydd ap Dafydd eventually bequeathed Tir Dol y Llan and the house adjoining "by the gret stone called y Maen Lloid" to his son Griffith ap Dafydd. The descendents of the family, which took the name Lloyd, of the Cardiganshire houses of Gilfachwen and Cilgwyn, continued to own the house until the beginning of the 18th century.[2]

Ownership thereafter is uncertain, but it is known that the Rev'd John Thomas, vicar of Llandysul and Llanllwni, lived there after 1744 and immediately before the arrival of Dr Stevenson the house was inhabited by a General James Morgan.[3] Dr David Stevenson, who is described by Thomas Lloyd as surely "the most overlooked member" of the social circle of Thomas Johnes of Hafod, arrived at Dôl-llan in the 1790s. Evidence about him is scanty and he escapes reference in all recent writings on Hafod, yet he was to Johnes, in a letter to George Cumberland "a particular friend of mine", whose projected departure from Dôl-llan, within ten years of his arrival, was a source of regret.[4]

Underlining this friendship more publicly was the commissioning by Johnes of a large group portrait by George Romney of members of the Johnes family with Major-General Lewis[5] and Dr Stevenson. This was lost in the 1807 fire at Hafod, but it appears in the list of art works at the mansion printed on Johnes' press earlier that year[6] and a watercolour copy is in the National

---

1. NLW Cilgwyn Deeds.
2. Francis Jones, *Historic Carmarthenshire Homes & their Familes*, Carmarthenshire Antiquarian Society/Dyfed County Council.
3. H. M. Vaughan, *Catalogue of Welsh Bookplates in the collection of Sir E. D. Jones, 1820*, p. 81.
4. Unpublished letter; British Library Add, MS 36498, f221.
5. Major [not General] William Lewis of Llanerchaeron.
6. NLW.

Library of Wales. This shows Stevenson having his palm read by Jane Johnes, perhaps a reference to the dilemma he soon faced about whether to stay in Wales or return to London. Stevenson's inclusion in that portrait is, as Thomas Lloyd says, "a compliment of high degree".

Stevenson was baptised on New Year's Day, 1743, the second son and fifth child of eight of David and Sarah Stevenson of Beaconsfield, Buckinghamshire. His parents were evidently well off as both brothers went to Eton and in 1761, aged 17, David entered Kings College, Cambridge. He gained a BA in 1765, MA in 1769 and received his LL.D. in 1778. A more signal mark of his ability is that no sooner had he completed his degree exams in 1764 than he was elected a Fellow of Kings, an honour he resigned in 1795. It was this year that he moved to Wales. On 27 October 1795 David Stephenson and his wife Judith signed up for a 500 year lease on Dôl-llan.[7]

Stevenson's chosen branch of the Law in indicated by his membership of Doctors' Commons. This was a select college of ecclesiastical lawyers, appointed by the Archbishop of Canterbury, and established in buildings near St Paul's Cathedral, which exercised a monopoly in certain aspects of civil and canon law, including the litigation of divorce and probate. It was abolished in 1857.

We have no way of knowing what brought Stevenson to Dôl-llan. It may be that he already knew Thomas Johnes and had a yen to try his own hand at agricultural and landscape improvement. He must have got to work without delay because within ten years he was back in London. The evidence for his early return comes in Johnes' letter to George Cumberland, already quoted above, which is dated 16 April 1798, where he tries to persuade his friend to buy Dôl-llan: "In my last I forgot to mention an exceeding pretty farm that is to be disposed of in this county. It is very romantically situated upon the banks of the Teify, on the opposite side of the water to Llandysil – so that in fact it is in Carmarthenshire. It is very well worth your seeing and I believe immediate possession may be had. It belongs to a particular friend of mine, who purchased it a few years ago, but whose family insist upon his residing nearer to them. It is with great regret he is forced to leave this Country. The house is convenient, tho' an old one patched up – but his farmyard and offices are very handsome. I think if you saw it, you would like the situation and perhaps would agree, for he is very liberal."

On 21 January 1799 Johnes wrote again to Cumberland: "There are two places you may have in this Country . . . The first is a farm of 220 acres upon the river Tivy, very beautiful and well cultivated, the house comfortable and convenient, a most excellent farmyard, which is to be sold. I imagine the price will be about 4 or 500£. There is wood upon it."[8]

Stevenson was not finally to sell until 1806, by which time the discerning and informative B. H. Malkin had visited – in 1803. He penned a glowing testimony:

> "Dr Stevenson's house is on the Caermarthenshire side of the river, in a style of neatness and simplicity well suited to the complexion of the spot. This gentleman, delighting in agricul-tural enterprises, has created a farm here, at his own very heavy cost, but with a degree of success that will amply repay his labour in the course of time. He is very sanguine, but not a miscalculating speculator. The estate is small, but in train of being improved to the utmost. The buildings and offices about the farm and house are models of ingenious contrivance for the purpose to which they are applied. They may perhaps rather exceed what the premises require but in every other respect they are perfect. The place has been much visited by those

7. NLW Morgan Richardson MSS, 1179 Dolellan Deeds.
8. R. Moore-Colyer, *A Land of Pure Delight*, 1992, p. 140.

who are curious in the practice of husbandry. It has equal attraction for the painter. The hanging wood above the garden, stretching itself parallel with the river, as far as the eye can reach, with the village and other circumstances, furnishes an admirable subject either for contemplation or the pencil."[9]

The following year, in 1804, Richard Fenton, a fellow member with Stevenson, of Doctors' Commons, called on his old acquaintance:

"Pursued our journey towards Llandyssil to call on Doctor Stephenson, whom I often met in London and elsewhere about sixteen years ago . . . Crossed the ford to Old Castle, formerly called Dôl-llan, the seat of Dr Stephenson who was from home. I left my name there and rode across his farm which he seems to manage in the English manner, his wheat being planted in rills and a large field preparing for Lucern. His farmyard of great extent on the summit and in the centre of his farm. Just above his house on a projecting knoll appears the vestiges of an old encampment."[10]

Dr Stevenson had left Dôl-llan by 1805 but still enjoyed a close connection with Llandysul. On June 3 that year, Eliza, daughter of Herbert Evans of Highmead, Llanybydder, and wife of David Lloyd of Alltyrodin, died at the age of 36. "Dr Stephenson, late of Dôl llan" composed a poem "out of affection and regard for Mrs Lloyd", which was inscribed on her white marble memorial in Llandysul parish church:

> Learn from her life the virtues that commend
> The Child, the Wife, the Parent, and the Friend
> Learn from her death, that Heavn's decrees ordain
> To Beauty and to Youth a short-liv'd reign.
> Then soar like her, releas'd from wordly cares,
> To bliss which God for purest souls prepares.[11]

In 1806 it was the estate agent's turn to describe Dôl-llan. An advertisement in *The Cambrian* of 28 June states that Oldcastle or "Dolans" near Llandysul is to be sold by auction. The advertisement describes a compact family house, lately enlarged and improved at considerable expense, with eight best bedchambers and a convenient farmhouse, yard and stable, barns, etc., "the whole being lately erected. No expense has been spared by the proprietor. It stands on the Teivy and comprises 240 acres".

The high standing of Dôl-llan, or as it was then being called in reference to the nearby encampment, Oldcastle,[12] is evident from the sale of a 500-year lease within a month by private treaty to a purchaser of status from far away.[13] This was a former Irish MP, George Agar, who was created

9. B. H. Malkin, *The Scenery, Antiquities, and Biography of South Wales*, 2nd edition, 1870. Vol. II, p. 150.
10. R. Fenton, *Tours in Wales (1804–13)*, 1917, p. 9.
11. S. R. Meyrick, *History of Cardiganshire*, London, T. Bewsley, 1808.
12. Oldcastle is used in the parish registers of this date. The small encampment overlooking the ancient ford of the river Teifi is described in the Royal Commission of Ancient Monuments for Carmarthenshire, 1917. No. 394, p. 133.
13. *The Cambrian*, 26 July 1806.

Lord Callan in 1790 and made a Representative Peer to Parliament in 1801. His Lordship's arrival in Llanfihangel-ar-Arth had an electrifying effect upon the vicar, Methusalem Williams, who devoted three long and carefully written lines in the church register to record the baptism of Lord Callan's son soon after the family took up residence at Dôl-llan. The effusive and sycophantic sentence contrasts with the perfunctory entries for those the vicar considered to be lesser mortals.[14]

In 1813 Dôl-llan was bought by John Morgan of London[15] and in 1824 John Thomas Morgan offered for sale "the former residence of Dr Stephens who built the same, and then the residence of Lord Callan."[16] However, Morgan was still living there in 1830, when he is listed as a J.P.[17] By 1835 a Captain H. J. Henley was living there. David Thomas of Llanfair bought the Dolellan [sic] estate on 1 April 1843.[18] He left it in his will to Rees Thomas and it stayed in the Thomas family until 1887 when the estate, totalling 750 acres, was sold at auction after the death of Capt David Thomas (1846–1882). The sale at the Porth Hotel on 16 August 1887 shows Dôl-llan recently "thoroughly repaired at considerable cost" as an exceedingly desirable, valuable and attractive freehold family residence" with just over 67 acres of "rich meadow and pasture land abutting on the river Teifi and an excellent grove of oak and other trees affording a most delightful residence. There are "capital" outbuildings including three coach-houses with a large granary over a "men's room", stables, barn, cow sheds, carthouse, boiler house and loft, and pigsties. The nine lots included Dolgrogws and 169 acres, Dôl-llan Ucha with 150 acres and Craig-Gwrth-Haiarn with 153 acres, a separate dwelling known as Penshingre, and Dolbantau – a five bedroom house and a "recently erected" large carding and spinning factory measuring 90ft by 21ft, let on a 60-year lease to William Davies. All nine lots, including Dôl-llan itself, had been mortgaged. The estate was sold to different buyers, separating Stevenson's model farmyard from the house.[19]

Dôl-llan was "in hand" at the time of the auction, unlike its acreage, which was let to several tenants. By the time of the 1891 census the house was occupied by the exotic-sounding Paget W. d'Estrange, a 50-year-old Ireland-born retired Colonel in the Royal Artillery, his wife Eliza, their two adult children – the son Perceval, a student at Oxford, and a daughter named Louisa – with a cook, housekeeper, housemaid and general male servant. Ten years later it was occupied by farm worker Jenkin Lloyd and his wife Mary and their teenage children. The eldest daughter Jane, aged 17, was a domestic servant.

The next resident we know about was Major Charles Herbert David Cass, DSO, who was born in 1858 at Arlington, Sussex, and died on June 24, 1929. He was buried in the graveyard at Llandysul. He moved to Dôl-llan at some time after he retired from the army in 1905 following a career that saw active service in the Boer War from 1899 to 1902. He was appointed a member of the Distinguished Service Order in 1900 and held The Queen's Medal with three clasps and two King's Medal with two clasps. Cass was High Sheriff of Cardiganshire in 1912–13.

A Conservative Church man, hunting and fishing were his favourite pastimes, and he used to spend two or three weeks of the year with the Tivyside and Neuadd Fawr hunts. He was frequently seen fishing the Teifi between March and May. He was said to be devoted to his home at Dôl-llan

14. Carmarthen Record Office, Llanfihangel ar Arth Parish Registers, 3 January 1807.
15. Op. cit., 2.
16. *Carmarthen Journal*, 21 May 1824, where he is incorrectly named John Morgan Thomas.
17. Carmarthen Record Office, Carmarthenshire Antiquarian Society Scrapbook, A20, Vol. III, p. 11.
18. Op. cit., 7 1179 Dolellan Deeds.
19. NLW Carmarthen Sale Catalogues 393.

and spent much of his time gardening. He patronised local horse races, the annual horse show, all athletic sports and local rifle clubs, being president and vice-president of each at various times. He was very fond of children, and frequently entertained picnics in the Dôl-llan demesne. School log-books relate his visits in one of the few early automobiles in the district, bearing oranges for the children. The whole town turned out for his burial.

Dôl-llan has always been a desirable residence in a picturesque setting. It sits under a hillside and a belt of trees, looking across the Teifi flood plain to Llandysul Church – thus its name, "church meadow". Its attraction to painters was a point well made by Malkin, as J. G. Wood for his *Rivers of Wales* (1813) sketched the view that Malkin described and Dôl-llan is conspicuous – the river in those days flowing close by the house.

As Johnes says, the house was already old when Stevenson arrived. He embellished what was no more than a plain two-storey farmhouse by moving the entrance to the western side, which he extended and made twin gabled, building a classical entrance porch between. J. G. Wood's sketch shows two plain two-storey buildings side by side with no central connection, though there is no way of knowing its accuracy. Under Stevenson's improvements the old front was transformed with two Venetian windows about the old front door, which became a round-headed window. Internally this became two principal rooms, connected by large double doors. The external plan makes a passing reference to John Nash and his design at Llanerchaeron for William Lewis, Thomas Johnes' first cousin. Thomas Lloyd observes that there is none of Nash's refinement, but he wonders whether Nash might have suggested the basic theme.

The farmyard that struck Malkin and Fenton is not by the house but, as Fenton says, on the summit of the estate to the north east. For long called Farmyard farm – Dôl-llan Ucha – this was the acme of Stevenson's achievement, but much of this was lost before the present owners came. The same fate has overtaken the lesser service buildings beside the house.

The farmyard is a spacious quadrangle containing, according to the 1887 sale catalogue (listed clockwise) a dwelling house, coal house, cattle sheds, cow houses, cart house with loft over, barn, stable, chaff room, root house and boiler house. Only one building of distinction remains today, though sliding into disrepair – a fine combined double cart house with loft over and barn with a single pair of large through doors, all under a graciously sloping slate hipped roof on original timbers. Instead of the usual ventilation slits, the barn is aired by a regular grid of small square openings, which run diagonally upward through the wall. This comparatively large and "ingeniously" built barn was to store the crops that Fenton saw, while a little way below is a now empty pond, which possibly was intended for a mill, of which no trace can be seen. More obvious are at least two fine shelter belts of mature beech, stretching away to protect the hilltop fields. In Stevenson's day the farmhouse was occupied by Thomas and Mary Nelson.[20] In Rees Thomas's time the tenants were David Evans aged 67 and his wife Mary, aged 63, their son John aged 42, another son aged 21 and three daughters, all unmarried.[21]

The property now accommodates the Farmyard nurseries, a plant enterprise led by Leicestershire-born Richard Bramley. The enterprise, which specialises in hellebores, has won gold awards at all the major Royal Horticultural Society shows in Britain, including Chelsea. As well as retail sales on site, the company has an outlet in Carmarthen market.

20. Carmarthen Record Office. Llanfihangel ar Arth Baptisms, 13 October 1805 and 30 November 1806 – children of Thomas and Mary Nelson of Oldcastle Farmyard.
21. Llanfihangel ar Arth Census, 1861.

Appendix 3

LLANFAIR

The fine old house of Llanfair is superbly situated on the Ceredigion side of the river Teifi opposite the ancient Iron Age hill fort of Craig Gwrtheyrn. The house itself has a four-bay stucco front added to a much earlier building *c.*1796,[1] after Thomas Thomas married Jane, daughter of Rev'd David Lloyd and sole heiress to the Llwynrhydowen and Brynllefrith estates. A further side addition was built *c.*1840, probably by his grandson, also called Thomas Thomas. It may originally have been part of a small settlement as an excavation in the field between the mansion and the river produced some medieval finds. There was once a chapel of ease, dedicated to Mair – Mary – on this site and Samuel Meyrick says each of the chapels of ease of Llandysul parish church, of which "Llanvair" was one, stood "in a separate hamlet".[2] The parish registers record three baptisms in Capel Llanfair, in 1722, 1724 and 1728.[3]

The house bears evidence of great longevity. There are possibly the remains of an Elizabethan fireplace in the oldest part, which became essentially the servants wing after the main improvements. The width of the walls alone testifies to its antiquity, but there is scant written evidence. Francis Jones[4] correctly assumed that it was also known as Llanfairperthycyndyn. Jones, who is unreliable on Dôl-llan, says Thomas ap David, younger son of David ap Rhys David Llewelyn Lloyd of Castell Hywel had a son, Rhys, alive in 1709, whose three daughters became co-heiresses. One of them, Margaret, Married her first cousin, Thomas David of Ffosesgob. Their elder son, David Thomas, succeeded to Ffosesgob and died without issue in 1758. The second son, Rhys Thomas, inherited Llanfair and married Gwenllian, daughter of John Evans of Gwarcoed Einon. Their eldest son was Thomas Thomas who married the heiress Jane Lloyd (the second son, John Thomas, inherited Ffosesgob). Thomas and Jane's eldest son was David Thomas, father of our diarist Rees.

Thomas Thomas found himself wealthy beyond all expectation after marrying Jane Lloyd. His brother John sold him Ffosesgob before emigrating to America and the marriage settlement dated 1778 brought him the Llwynrhydowen and Pantydefaid estates on the death of his father-in-law the following year, though there must have been some provision for David Lloyd's second wife Letitia, who lived until 1812, and who bore him five children. By 1796 Thomas had added the mansion's distinctive frontage with its wide and gracious entrance hall accessing spacious drawing and dining rooms on each side, and, a year later according to date stones on the buildings, the model farmyard quadrangle. Thomas married again after his wife Jane's death, in 1804, to Anne David of Penallt-tycwple, of the neighbouring parish of Bangor. The date of his death is not known,

---

1. Lloyd, Orbach & Scourfield, *The Buildings of Wales – Carmarthenshire & Ceredigion (Pevsner)*, Yale University Press , 2006.
2. S. R. Meyrick, *History of Cardiganshire*, London, 1808.
3. Rev'd W. J. Davies, *Hanes Plwyf Llandyssul*, J. D. Lewis, Llandyssul, 1896.
4. *Historic Cardiganshire Homes & their Families*, Brawdy Books, 2000.

Old Lodge Dôl-llan.
(Old postcard, courtesy of Thomas Lloyd).

Dôl-llan from Llandysul Parish Church.
(Photograph: Steve Dubé).

The Drive, Dôl-llan.
(Old postcard, courtesy of Thomas Lloyd).

Dôl-llan: the old front.
(Photograph courtesy of Tom Lloyd).

Dôl-llan close up, 2003.
(Photograph: Steve Dubé).

Dôl-llan painting (of watercolour by unknown artist).
(Photograph: Steve Dubé).

Dôl-llan main staircase.
(Photograph: Steve Dubé).

Dôl-llan drawing room.
(Photograph: Steve Dubé).

Dôl-llan dining room.
(Photograph: Steve Dubé).

Dôl-llan – Major Cass burial – June 1929.

Meet of the Neuadd Fawr Foxhounds at Dôl-llan, c.1910.
(Old postcard, courtesy of Thomas Lloyd).

Church schools treat at Dôl-llan (old postcard).

Llanfair (painting by unknown artist).

Llanfair.
(Photograph: Steve Dubé).

Llanfair clock.
(Photograph: Steve Dubé).

Date stone on house, Llanfair,
Thomas Thomas, 1796.
(Photograph: Steve Dubé).

Date stone on outbuildings at Llanfair,
Thomas Thomas, 1797.
(Photograph: Steve Dubé).

Llanfair chapel entrances.
(Photograph: Steve Dubé).

Date stone on house at Llanfair –
Thomas & Mary Thomas, 1847.
(Photograph: Steve Dubé).

Llanfair.

Llanfair aerial view.

but by 1818 his son David Thomas was in possession of Llanfair. The Tithe Rent Charge of 1841 shows a Llanfair estate of 16 properties and 1,172 acres.[5] When David Thomas died on 1 August 1845 the Llanfair house with 192 acres and its substantial estate was inherited by his eldest son Thomas Thomas, the diarist's brother. He carried out the last significant refurbishments of the mansion, including a distinctive chapel, with a small vestry. The chapel had separate staircases and entrances for family and servants. These extensive improvements included a new four-bay frontage with off-centre gable.[6] This work may have taken a good decade to complete. In his diary entry recording the funeral of his brother Thomas Thomas in February 1860, Rees Thomas writes that Thomas had made *"a fine place"* of Llanfair but *"as soon as he had completed the great improvements there [he] was summoned by the cold hand of death to quit it for ever."* This observation appears at odds with a date stone on the mansion that suggests the refurbishments were complete in 1847. It may be that the internal refurbishments, including chapel and vestry, took longer. Thomas also commissioned the oak longcase (grandfather) clock from Henry Jones of Llandysul, who was said to be self-taught, itinerant and a poet.[7] The clock is thought to have been made for the new library at Llanfair.[8]

Thomas Thomas also increased the estate in June 1845 by spending £3,794 on five properties in the parish of Llanfihangel ar Arth – Blaenwaun, Graig, Graig Fach, Llwynbedw and Frongoch – totalling 242 acres.[9] When Thomas Thomas died in 1860 he left a will leaving the estate to his eldest son David on his 25th birthday (10 October 1871) and securing legacies for all his other children from Llanfair the rents of another 25 properties in Llandysul, Llanwenog, Llanybydder and Pencarreg. The whole issue ended up in Chancery and was only settled in 1873 after lengthy litigation.[10]

David Thomas was a captain in the Cardiganshire Militia, who supported his lifestyle through a succession of mortgages. It was Captain David Thomas who evicted four of his tenants – Thomas Thomas of Pantydefaid, David Thomas of Cwmmarch, Morris of Ddolgou and William Jones of Caerau – in the notorious *Y Gorthrymedigion* – The Oppressed – scandal after they voted for the Liberal candidate instead of the Tory in the 1868 general election.[11] Henry Richards, the Tregaron-born MP, told Parliament that he knew of 43 such evictions in Cardiganshire and 26 in Carmarthenshire.

The *Landowners Return* of 1873 shows David Thomas of Llanfair with an estate of 2,520 acres and an annual rental of £1,204. Captain Thomas and his brother John (who in fact died in 1870) were assigned a coat of arms in 1974, with the motto *Clemens et Verax* – Merciful and Truthful, the year Captain David Thomas was High Sheriff of Cardiganshire. He died in 1882 and left the estate in his will to the Rev'd James Jones, former vicar of Llanfihangel ar Arth and by then vicar of Clydey in Pembrokeshire, and the lawyer James John Chapman of London. The estate by now totalled 1,521 acres and yielded annual rents of £815. It was gradually auctioned off piecemeal in 1884, 1899 and finally the mansion itself in 1908, by which time it was unoccupied.[12]

5. Leslie Baker-Jones, *Princelings, Privilege and Power*, Gomer, 1999, p. 162.
6. Ibid., Lloyd, Orbach & Scourfield.
7. Richard Bebb, *Welsh Furniture 1250–1950*, Vol. Two, Saer Books, 2007.
8. Richard Bebb, ibid., believes the clock originally had pad feet, which would have made it too tall for its present position in the hall at Llanfair. It was returned to the mansion by the present owners, John and Gwenllian Kidd.
9. NLW Morgan Richardson MS 1110.
10. NLW Ibid., MS 1198.
11. Ibid., Rev'd W. J. Davies.
12. NLW Ibid., MSS 1311, 1316, 1426, 1436.

The sale catalogue of 1908 described Llanfair as "an exceptionally attractive estate of a very sporting character", with a southern aspect on the north bank of the river Teifi with a "brinkage" – presumably river frontage – of about one and a quarter miles with one of the best salmon pools of the river. There are three large riverside meadows and 41 acres of woodland, mostly "ripe for cutting". The meets of the Tivy-side Foxhounds and the Neuaddfawr Foxhounds are within easy reach.

"The mansion house is conveniently situated in the centre of the property, and sheltered by the surrounding plantations. It is of convenient size and contains the following accommodation, viz.:– On the Ground Floor, Spacious Entrance Hall, Drawing Room, Dining Room, Library, or Smoking Room, Gun Room, Kitchens, Servants' Hall, Laundry, Dairy, Larder, Store Room, Boiling House, etc., with good Wine and Beer Cellars in basement, and on the Upper Floor, Seven Bedrooms, Four Dressing Rooms, Two Bathrooms, Lavatory, W.C., etc."

Outside there is a water-driven turbine operating farm machinery, stabling for eight horses, a coach-house and three rooms for a coachman. The "most substantially built" quadrangle of farm buildings, built as "a Model Farm Yard regardless of cost" includes a 16-tie cow-house, further stabling for six horses, cart-houses, large barn and granary, stock sheds and "piggeries".

The first resident following the Thomas family was Captain Arthur Connop Newland of Devon, who rented the mansion for nine years from the trustees of the late David Thomas for £70. In 1940 it was inherited by Mrs Gladys Douglas from her fiancé the Rev'd Cyril Moore, who had bought it in 1938. Mrs Douglas started the Teifi herd of Jersey cattle in 1943. In 1956 she married Alec Fraser, who died three years later. When she died in 1974 she bequeathed the place to her niece, Gwenllian Kidd, who has lived there since 1976, when her husband Captain John Kidd, retired from the Royal Navy.

I am indebted to Gwenllian Kidd for her help in compiling this appendix.

Biographical Index
of People and Characters

[Close family in **CAPITAL LETTERS**]

Amphlett, James: Aged 35, of Black Lion, Llandysul, described as "fund holder". Born Birmingham, *c*.1826. His wife Hannah was a native of Llandysul. They had a ten-month-old daughter, Caroline. [*1861 Census, Llandyssil.*]

Barker, John Hoyes: John Hoyes Barker, Carmarthen-based solicitor who also served as clerk of the peace for Carmarthen borough and registrar of the diocese of St Davids. Born Grenada, West Indies. Father of Thomas William Barker (1861–1912).

Beynon, Jenkin: Uncle of **Mary**, the deceased wife of Rees's brother **Thomas**. Extremely rich. He owned property in the parishes of Llaneraeron, Henfynyw, Llanllwchairn, Llandisiliogogo, Ciliau Aeron, Dihewid, Llanfihangel Ystrad and Llangrannog, including the Ship Inn and village shop. JBE died 2 February 1849. His will, which left legacies to support two local schools as well as sums of money to members of the Thomas family, was the subject of a protracted case in Chancery that dragged on until 1870. [*Morgan Richardson Papers, 1128 et al, NLW.*]

Davies, Evan: One of the Dôl-llan farm servants, aged 25.

Davies, Rev'd John, "Dancoed": Born 1836 at Tancoed, Llanwenog. Died 1922. Minister of Alltyblacca, Capel Bryn and Sychpant. Missionary. Kept a grammar school at Cwrtnewydd for 20 years. [Rev'd David Evans, *Welsh Unitarians as Schoolmasters*, J. D. Lewis Sons, published post-1904.]

Davies family of Llangunllo: Dr Thomas Davies, Rector of Llangynllo. Born *c*.1807. Married Rees's sister **Margaret Thomas**. Their children included Susannah Gwenllian (known as Anne), born *c*.1852, who married R. T. P. Williams, a solicitor of Haverfordwest, and who is understood to have lodged this diary in the Record Office at Haverfordwest. Other children were David, Johnny, Grace, Mary Jane and Frances Louisa.

Davis, David, "Serv't Llanfair": Aged 36 in 1861, married to Deborah, aged 30. One son, Rees, aged nine. [*1861 Census, Llandyssil.*]

Davis, Dr: Henry Harries Davies was born in Llanwenog in 1836, son of James and Mary (Harries) Davies and brought up largely on his maternal grandmother's farm of Pantfen, Llanfihangel ar

Arth. He was probably at home sleeping on the night of August 26, 1843, when a gang of Rebecca rioters, armed with guns and reaping hooks, dragged his grandfather Daniel Harries from his bed, forced him to sign off his claim to a disputed will and ransacked the house. H. H. Davies completed his training in 1858 and went into practice in Llandysul, where he lived and practised at Rock House. Later became more widely known as the family doctor of the Welsh Fasting Girl Sarah Jacob of Llethrneuadd, Llanfihangel ar Arth. He died in January 1931. [Harold Selcon, *The Changing Face of Medicine in 20th Century Llandysul*, Gomer, 2002; *1841 Census, Llanfihangel ar Arth*; Pat Molloy, *And They Blessed Rebecca*, Gomer, 1983, et al.]

Davis, Mr Lloyd: John Lloyd Davies of Alltrodyn and Blaendyffryn, Llandysul. Born 1801 in the Black Lion, Aberystwyth, lawyer and magistrate, Deputy Lieutenant of Cardiganshire and Carmarthenshire and Conservative MP for Cardigan Borough. Died in 1860.

Davis William Gilfachwen: William Davies of Gilfachwen Ucha, aged 34, a farmer of 105 acres employing three labourers. [*1861 Census, Llandyssil.*]

Dio Farm: See **Evans, David**.

Dio Ffynnonbwla: See **Titus, David**.

Elliott, Thomas: "Capt Elliott": Thomas Elliott (*c.*1824–1870) of Dolhaidd Ucha, Penboyr.

Evan, David union: David Evans, born *c.*1822, schoolmaster, lived with his parents John, 66, inn keeper, and Mary, 62, and his sister Catherine, 28, at Union Tavern, Llandysul. [*1861 Census, Llandyssil.*]

Evans, David: "Dio Farm". Aged 67, farmer of 135 acres at Dolellan Uchaf (now Farmyard), married to Mary, with two sons and five daughters. [*1861 Census, Llandyssil.*]

Evans Edward, Abercerdin: Aged 42, registrar of births & deaths and a farmer of 60 acres. Unmarried and lives with his brother Evan. [*1861 Census, Llandyssil.*]

Evans, Evan, Nantcoch: Aged 40 and unmarried, a watchmaker and engraver who lived with his widowed mother Elinor, 72, a seamstress and laundress and his sister Esther, also 40 and also a seamstress and laundress, his mother's nephew, David Thomas, aged 18, an apprentice carpenter and Sarah Jones, 16, apprentice seamstress. [*1861 Census, Llanfihangel ar Arth.*]

Evans, the Rev'd Evan (1820–1863): of Llaethlliw in the parish of Henfynyw, Aberaeron and Cwrt Farm, Llanwenog, second son of **John Evans** of Court (Cwrt) Farm & Anne Beynon, sister of **Jenkin Beynon** of Llaethlliw (1778–1849). Evan Evans was brother of the late Mary Thomas and brother-in-law of Rees' elder brother **Thomas Thomas**. His elder brother was David Beynon Evans (1817–1855). Both Evan Evans and his brother died without issue. Evan mortgaged Llaethlliw for £25,000 on 25 June 1863. He died on 27 December, 1863.

Evans, John (Mr Evans Court Farm), of Cwrtnewydd, Llanwenog, "Old Man Cwrt", "Old Evans Court farm", etc. Married Anne Beynon (d.1845), daughter of David Beynon and Mary (née Evans) and sister of **Jenkin Beynon Evans**; their children were **Mary**, who married Rees' brother **THOMAS THOMAS**, David Beynon Evans (1817–1855), and the **Rev'd Evan Evans**.

Evans, John: Shoemaker who lived at Upper Barley Mount in Llandysul. Aged 40, he employed three men in 1861.

Evans, the Rev'd John (1835–1888): Born Felinfach, Lampeter, educated at Rhydowen Grammar School and Carmarthen College. Minister at Gellionnen, 1862–1884. School teacher at various times in Llanybydder, Llwynygroes, Llidiadnennog, and for 25 years at Trebanos.

Evans, Rev'd T.: The Rev'd Titus Evans, Unitarian Minister and school teacher, former parish clerk at Llandysul and former solicitor's clerk in Llandysul and Swansea. He ran a school at Parcyfelfed, Carmarthen, from 1849 until his death at the age of 54 in 1864. [*Y Bywgraffiadur Cymreig Hyd 1940*, William Lewis Cyf., Caerdydd.]

Fitzwilliams, Edward Crompton Lloyd (1807–1880): Radically minded lawyer and squire of the Cilgwyn estate, Llandyfriog.

Griffith, Rev'd David, Tavistock (1823–1878): Born in Llandysul. Religious writer; Unitarian Minister in Llandeilo (1843–49), where he also ran a school. Also served as Minister at Aberdeen, 1849–53, Wareham, 1854–58, Tavistock, 1858–66, and Cheltenham, 1866–78. He published several works, all in English, the most important being *The Continuity of Religious Development*, 1867. [D. Elwyn Davies; *Eminent Welshmen: T. R. Roberts. A short biographical dictionary of Welshmen who have attained distinction from the earliest times to the present*, The Educational Publishing Company Ltd., 1906.]

Griffiths, E.: Evan Griffiths, aged 44 in 1861, a farmer of 168 acres at Dolgrogwys, the farm adjoining Dôl-llan. A tenant of Rees Thomas and his best friend, Griffiths is married to Mary and they have a daughter, Elizabeth, aged 12 and a son, John, aged 9. Griffiths employs three "boys" – farm servants, and there are two domestic servants. [*1861 Census, Llandyssil.*]

James, Mrs, Wilks Head: Hanna James, 38, wife of John James, 39, farmer of 140 acres and inn keeper at the Wilkes Head. They have two sons and a household consisting of a ploughman, cowman, dairy maid, housemaid and bar maid and a kitchen maid. [*1861 Census, Llanfihangel ar Arth.*]

James Rev'd J.: The Rev'd John James (1779–1864). Born Llangeler. Former Minister at Pantydefaid, where he was eventually buried. A former close friend and colleague of the Rev'd John Thomas (qv). Persuaded by Iolo Morganwg to move to Gellionnen in the Swansea Valley and kept a boarding school at his home in Vardre, Clydach. [Rev'd David Evans, *Welsh Unitarians as Schoolmasters*, J. D. Lewis & Sons, published post-1904.]

James, Walter, "Watty": Aged 38, Dôl-llan farm servant and tenant of Dôl-llan Lodge, where he lived with his wife Anne, 37. [*1861 Census, Llanfihangel ar Arth.*]

Jenkins, Mr, solicitor, Cardigan: Probably R. D. Jenkins, Solicitor, Cardigan (subsequently Messrs Jenkins & Evans).

Jones the Shop: A Margaret Jones, widow, kept a shop at 21 King Street and employed seven people (she also had a farm of 41 acres) in 1851. Four people worked in the shop, including her daughter Mary. Mrs Jones was 50 in 1851 and Mary 23. Another daughter, Anne, was 13. For some reason neither this large shop, nor Mrs Jones, were listed in the 1861 Census. [*1851 Census, Llandyssil.*]

Jones, Dr: Dr John Jones of Tyssul Lodge, practised in Llandysul from *c.*1851. Died aged 69 in 1870. Dr Jones, Lodge's wife was Eliza, also 41. [*1861 Census, Llandyssil*; Harold Selcon, *The Changing Face of Medicine in 20th Century Llandysul*, Gomer, 2002.]

Jones, Mr, Penlan: David Jones, aged 45, a farmer of 146 acres. [*1861 Census, Llandyssil.*]

Jones, David, pensioner, alias **Serg't Jones, Nantygragen**. The Jones family lived at Nantygragen in Llanfihangel ar Arth parish for 30 years from the first census, but there was no record of a David Jones.

Jones, Enoch: of Blaenmain, Llanfihangel ar Arth, aged 22 in 1861, son of Elizabeth Jones, aged 58, widow, hose knitter & pauper. One of the young men who came courting Rees' servant Anne.

Jones, Miss Jane, Nantremenyn: Aged 43, an unmarried laundress. She has a servant, Mary Davies, aged 32. [*1861 Census, Llandyssil.*]

Jones, John (1834–1884) Gelli Faharen: The Thomas family solicitor, and there was a close family connection. He was a son of David Jones of Gellifaharen and his wife Jane, whose mother was a granddaughter of Dafydd Dafis of Castell Howell. A grandmother was Mary Thomas, sister of the diarist's grandfather Thomas Thomas. He was killed in July 1884 after a day out in Aberystwyth as they returned by their own carriage from New Quay Road railway station (Llanfihangel ar Arth). The horse bolted as they made their way down Wesley Hill. The carriage failed to turn the corner and Jones and his governess, a Miss Howell, were both fatally injured. [H. R. Evans, 'A Village Worthy', *Ceredigion*, Vol. IV, No. 2, 1961.]

Jones, Rev'd John, Blaenannerch: Rev'd John Jones (1807–1875), Calvinistic Methodist minister; b. 4 Oct. 1807 at Melin Blaenpistyll, Llangoedmor, son of Samuel and Charlotte Jones. While still very young, his parents went to live at Cytir-bach, near Blaenannerch. He was given a little education in the local day school and later in a school at Cardigan. His interest in preaching started when he was a boy, and in 1833, after experiencing a profound religious emotion, he himself began to preach. He soon made a name for himself and began to tour the country as was usual in those days. He was ordained at the Llangeitho Association in 1841. In 1842 he married Mrs James of Canllufaes, and lived at that place and at Cytir-bach until he built his own house near Blaenannerch. He was in the field for over forty years, and no one in Wales was held in higher esteem, in Associations or other preaching-festivals, than 'Old Blaenannerch', as he was called. His resonant voice and sweeping, fiery eloquence dominated his congregations everywhere. He died 14 January 1875 and was buried in front of Blaenannerch chapel. [J. E. Lloyd (editor), *Dictionary of Welsh Biography down to 1940*, University of Wales Press.]

Jones, Mrs, Gelliffaren: Jane Jones of Gelli Faharen, aged 49, mother of John Jones solicitor. Granddaughter of the Rev'd Dafydd Dafis, the poet and teacher of Castell Hywel, Pontsian.

Jones Richard: Described as a curate living at Vaedrefawr. Not listed in the census as living in Faerdre Fawr. Neither is he listed as a curate at Llandysul.

Jones, Rev'd James Kilsby: James Rhys Kilsby Jones (1813–1889), Congregational minister at Rhayader at this time (1857–60), regarded as one of the most notable men of his period – 'famous' in the eyes of his admirers but 'odd' in those of his critics. He was different from other people in his mode of life, his dress, his manner of expressing himself; his personality may also be described as most original. Rules, regulations, accepted modes, and customs – he was above all such things. In his personality bravery and gentleness were combined. He hated all deceit and hypocrisy. He wrote much to weekly and denominational journals; he also brought out (1867) an edition of the works of William Williams of Pantycelyn. [*Rev'd John Dyfnallt Owen, M.A. (1873–1956), Aberystwyth*, Welsh Biography Online.]

Jones, Rev'd Rees, Aberdar: Rees Jenkin Jones (1835–1924) Unitarian minister, schoolmaster, historian, and hymn-writer. [*The Dictionary of Welsh Biography Down to 1940*, The Honourable Society of Cymmrodorion, 1959.]

Jones, William: Mr Jones, Llwyngroes: Aged 32, Squire of Llwyngroes, Llanwnnen, landowner and magistrate and farmer of 150 acres. [*1861 Census, Llanwnen*; Francis Jones, *Historic Cardiganshire Homes and their Families*, Brawdy Books, 2000.]

Lewis Mr, Cwmbychan: I believe this refers to Lewis Evans, 35, of Cwmbychan, a 65-acre farm. [*1861 Census, Llanfihangel ar Arth.*]

Lewis, Ann, Nantegryd: one of the servants of Rees's brother **Evan** at Nantegryd.

Lewis, Capt: Captain William Price Lewes, Llysnewydd, Llangeler (1813–1890). Old gentry family, also owned Duffryn, Llandybie, and later Llanerchaeron, near Aberaeron. High Sheriff of Carmarthenshire in 1860. Annual income of between £4,000 and £5,000.

Lewis, David: One of the enumerators of the 1861 census in Llandysul. The most likely candidate is David Lewis, aged 39, an unmarried stone engraver, who lives at Rhydowen End, who proves to be a stalwart assistant to Rees Thomas in helping to handle the family paperwork. [*1861 Census, Llandyssil.*]

Lloyd, Dr David: Dr David Lloyd (1805–1863), Professor from 1833 at Carmarthen College and Principal from 1835 until his death. Founder of Parcyvelvet Chapel, Carmarthen, known as The

College Chapel. A grandson of David Lloyd (1724–1779) of Brynllefrith, Llanwnnen, he was thus a relative (Rees and his brothers were great-grandsons of David Lloyd of Brynllefrith). Married in 1853 to Ellen, daughter of Stephen Smith of Swainby, Yorkshire. They had two children, David Lewis Lloyd and Lucy Lloyd, later Theakston. [Rev'd David Evans, *Welsh Unitarians as Schoolmasters*, J. D. Lewis & Sons, undated, p. 27; George Eyre Evans (editor), *Lloyd Letters*, 1908.]

Lloyd, John, Gilfachwen: Son of the Rev'd Thomas Lloyd, Rector of Llanfair Orllwyn. In 1861 John Lloyd was a 24-year-old law student. [*1861 Census, Llandyssil.*]

Lloyd, Rev'd Thomas: of Gilfachwen, Llandysul. Born *c.*1803. Rector of Llanfair Orllwyn. Gilfachwen Isaf is a farm of 200 acres. Magistrate. Married to Martha, born *c.*1813 in Glamorgan. Their daughters (ages on census night 7/8 April 1861 are: Mary, 25; Jane, 21; Anna, 20; Frances Margaret, 10. They also have two sons at home – John, 24 a law student and Richard Llewellin, aged 7.

Marles, Gwilym: The Rev'd William Thomas (1834–1879), Unitarian Minister, poet, editor and school teacher in Llandysul, great-uncle of Dylan Thomas.

Montalembert: Have been unable to trace this person, who appears to have been an agent or solicitor. It might be a nickname.

Morris, Lewis: Lewis Edward Williams Morris (1797–1872), solicitor of Mount Pleasant, later Penbryn, Llangunnor, father of the poet and author Lewis Morris. [Francis Jones, *Historic Carmarthenshire Homes & their Families*, p. 146.]

Parry, Tom A.: Thomas Parry, blacksmith, 46, lived with his widowed mother Margaret at Frongoch. [*1861 Census, Llandyssil.*]

Phillips, Dr of Newcastle (Emlyn): Believed to be Dr John Phillips.

Price, John Lloyd (1803–1865), of Glangwili, Llanllawddog, a magistrate.

Pryse, John Pugh Vaughan: Mr Pryse, Bwlchbychan (1818–1903), third son of Pryse Pryse of Gogerddan. [Francis Jones, *Historic Cardiganshire Homes & their Families*, Brawdy Books, 2000]; Herbert Vaughan in *South Wales Squires* wrote: "His residence reflected clearly his own tastes . . . in the dining room alone were to be seen some thirty foxes' masks, varied by a few heads of hares and otters' poles. Near the hearth-rug lay a footstool composed of a complete stuffed fox."

Rees, James (Wynllan): Aged 62, parish clerk, lived at Winllan with his wife Margaret. [*1861 Census, Llandyssil.*]

Rees, John, Penalltgerdyn: Aged 29, unmarried, butcher, lived with unmarried sister Mary, 24. [*1861 Census, Llanfihangel ar Arth.*]

Spurrell, William (1813–1889): Printer, publisher and local historian, whose business operated from King Street, Carmarthen, for nearly 100 years from 1841. [Joyce & Victor Lodwick, *The Story of Carmarthen,* 1953.

Titus, David (David Carp't Ffynnonbwla): Aged 40, carpenter. Lived at Ffynnonbwla with his wife Rachel, 39, and their children, son David, 17, and daughters Dinah, 13, Sarah, 9, Elizabeth, 4. [*1861 Census, Llanfihangel ar Arth.*]

Thomas, Mr, Rhydowen: David Thomas, aged 48, who kept the shop at Rhydowen with his brother William and sister Hannah. No relation. [*1861 Census, Llandyssil.*]

Rees, Thomas (Twmi Daniel): Tailor. Son of Daniel Rees, also a tailor, and his wife Susannah. In 1851 he was aged 30 and lived with his parents, both aged 66, at 22 King Street with his brother Daniel, 34, sisters Mary (43) and Sarah (28) and two of his nephews, David Davies (13) and William Thomas (6). [*1851 Census, Llandyssil.*]

Thomas, Ann: "Servant Ann", aged 23, who Rees Thomas employs as his house servant. She is hired on 15 October 1860 and leaves Dôl-llan on 19 November 1861.

THOMAS, ANNE (Annie) of Llanfair. Born 15 May 1845, eldest daughter of **THOMAS & MARY THOMAS** of Llanfair. Married Evan Jones of Tyssul Castle. Their children were David Thomas Jones, died aged 5 months on 7 August 1873; John Thomas Jones, died aged 3 years, 15 January 1878; Mary, who married John Henry Hywel Williams and had issue.

THOMAS, DAVID (1), (23 April 1825 to 29 October 1876): "Br David", a younger brother. A lawyer who was mentally unstable and who died in a lunatic asylum at Carmarthen. [*Ceredigion*, Vol. IV, No. 2, p. 172.]

Thomas, David (2), David Thomas, Rhydowen: Undertaker: Age 48, he kept Rhydowen Shop with his brother William and their sister Hannah. [*1861 Census, Llandyssil.*]

THOMAS, DAVID (3), (10 October 1846–23 February 1882): Eldest son of **THOMAS & MARY THOMAS** of Llanfair and the diarist's nephew. The *Landowners Return* of 1873 describes him as having an estate of 2,560 acres with a rental of £1,204. He was a magistrate, a Captain in the Cardiganshire Militia and High Sheriff of Cardiganshire in 1874. A coat of arms was assigned to David and his brother John in 1874. Understood to be the writer of the Child's Diary (Appendix). He died a bachelor, 23 February 1882. He was the last of the Thomas family to live at Llanfair.

THOMAS, EVAN (12 September 1830–5 November 1864) of Nantegryd: "Br Evan" – The youngest brother. He mortgaged his estate for the sum of £25,000. A heavy drinker, his death certificate describes him as a landed proprietor and the cause of death – at Dôl-llan – as angina pectoris. A brief obituary in *The Welshman* (11 November 1864) reads: "*He was a good neighbour and a liberal contributor towards the necessities of the poor in his locality. His memory will doubtless be long cherished in the bosoms of a wide circle of acquaintances.*"

THOMAS, JANE, born 27 June 1856 at Llanfair, daughter of **THOMAS THOMAS**. Married the Rev'd James Jones, vicar of Llandybie. They had two sons and two daughters. [*D/Wil/220.*]

THOMAS, JENKIN (Br Jenkin), born 31 March 1828: Lived at Tyssul Castle (now Cae'r Bryn, Llandysul). Never married. Later known as Jenkin Jones Thomas. A Captain in the Cardiganshire Militia. Died 30 May 1880 at 2 Beach Road, Weston Super Mare, having moved there "some time before". [*D/Wil/220.*]

JOHN THOMAS (1) (10 September 1819–17 March 1858): Surgeon. An older brother, who died without issue two years before Rees started his diary. Lived at Tyssul Castle.

THOMAS, JOHN (2), "Johnny", son of **THOMAS THOMAS** (1817–1860), born 24 May 1852 at Llanfair.

Thomas, John (3), the Rev'd: "The Rev'd & respected Mr J. Thomas, Blacklion" (1784–1861). No relation. Born Abergwili. Minister at Pantydefaid 1813 to 1847. Kept a grammar school at Llandysul until shortly before his death. [Rev'd David Evans, *Welsh Unitarians as Schoolmasters*, J. D. Lewis & Sons, undated.]

THOMAS, MARGARET: "Sishi", the diarist's only sister. Born 20 September 1814, she married the Rev'd **THOMAS HOWELL DAVIES** (died 1870), Rector of Llangynllo (Llangunllo). Their children are **GRACE, ANNE (Susanna Gwenllian), FRANCES LOUISA, MARY JANE, DAVID & JOHNNY**.

Thomas, John, Shopnewydd: John David Thomas, 39, draper, grocer and ironmonger of "New Shop". [*1861 Census, Llandyssil.*]

THOMAS, MARY (1). The diarist's mother. She was the daughter of John & Susannah Edwards of "Wernmagwith (Gwernmacwyyd), Llanfihangel ar Arth. She was a niece of the poet Thomas Edwards – Twm o'r Nant. At the time of her marriage settlement to **David Thomas** of Llanfair, her father John Edwards lived at Friars Park, Carmarthen. She died in 19 September 1876 at the age of 89. [*D/Wil/220.*]

THOMAS, MARY (2). Born 6 April 1848, died 8 August 1868 at Llanfair Hall, of consumption.

Thomas, Mary (3). The late wife of **THOMAS THOMAS**: **Mary Thomas**, née Evans, was daughter of **John Evans** of Court Farm, Cwrtnewydd, and his wife Ann (daughter of **Jenkin Beynon**).

REES THOMAS (1) (3 May 1823–8 November 1865): The Diarist, of **Dôl-llan**. Third son of David Thomas (1784–1 August 1845) of **Llanfair** and **Mary**.

Thomas, Rees (2) (Mr R. Cribor): Aged 30, auctioneer, lived with parents John and Jane Thomas at Cribor Fawr, a farm of 118 acres, and brother of Thomas Thomas (37), a Unitarian Minister. No relation. [*1861 Census, Llandyssil.*]

Thomas, Rees (3) (Uncle Ffoshelig): brother of Rees' father **David**. Rees Thomas inherited Ffoshelyg (Ffoshelig) a 232-acre holding from his father **Thomas Thomas**. He married Anne (Nancy), daughter of a Richards of Glanwern. [*D/Wil/220, Llandysul Tithe Map, 1841.*]

Thomas, Rev'd T.: Thomas Thomas (1824–1908) (no relation), Minister of Pantydefaid Chapel, Prengwyn, from 1847 to 1895. Founded Rhydowen Grammar Schools at Pontsian in 1847 and ran it for 30 years. [D. Elwyn Davies, *They Thought for Themselves, J. D. Lewis & Sons*, 1982, pp.44-45; Rev'd David Evans, *Welsh Unitarians as Schoolmasters*, J. D. Lewis & Sons, undated, p. 14.]

THOMAS, THOMAS (8 April 1817–11 February 1860): Of Llanfair (also known as Llanfairperthycyndyn). Rees' eldest brother, and the only one of the six to marry. Like all Rees' brothers he is usually prefixed "Br" in the text. Thomas married Mary Evans, daughter of **JOHN EVANS** of Court Farm, Llanwenog, by Anne Beynon, sister of Jenkin Beynon (1778–1849) of Llaethlliw near Aberaeron. Mary died shortly after giving birth on 2 July, 1856, at the age of 40. Their children were (1) **ANNE (Annie) THOMAS**, born 15 May 1845; (2) **DAVID THOMAS**, born 10 October 1848; (3) **MARY THOMAS**, born 6 April 1849; (4) **JOHNNY THOMAS**, born 24 May 1853; (5) **JANE THOMAS**, born 27 June 1856. [*D/Wil/220.*]

Thomas, Rev'd William: See also Gwilym Marles. In 1861 he was 26 and lived at Marblestone Hall with his wife Mary, 30 and their daughter Deanah Allan Thomas, aged six months. No relation. [*1861 Census, Llandyssil.*]

Wallop, Capt: Barter Wallop, aged 46, born London, was a lodger at the Old Black Lion, Llandysul, at the time of the census in April, 1861.

Watty: See James, Walter.

Williams, David: Kept the Kings Head Inn with his widowed mother Hannah, aged 68, and his widowed sister, aged 40. [C. H. R. Evans, *Ceredigion*, Vol. IV, No. 2, 1961.]

Bibliography

And They Blessed Rebecca, Pat Molloy. Gomer, 1983.

Cardiganshire County History, Volume 3. Cardiganshire Antiquarian Society/RCAHMS, 1998.

Carmarthenshire Antiquary (H. R. Evans), Vol. III, Parts 3 & 4, 1961.

Ceredigion, Journal of the Cardiganshire Antiquarian Society (H. R. Evans) Vol. I (2), 1951; Vol. III (2), 1957; Vol. IV (2), 1961.

Crafts, Customs and Legends of Wales, Mary Corbett Harris. David & Charles, 1970.

Hanes Plwyf Llandyssul, W. J. Davies. J. D. Lewis, Gwasg Gomer, 1896.

Hanes Plwyfi Llangeler a Phenboyr, Daniel E. Jones. J. D. Lewis, Gomerian Press, 1899.

Historic Cardiganshire Homes and their Families, Caroline Charles-Jones (editor). Brawdy Books, 2000.

Historic Carmarthenshire Homes and their Families, Francis Jones. Carmarthenshire Antiquarian Society/ Cultural Services Department, Dyfed County Council, 1987.

History of Cardiganshire, Samuel Rush Meyrick. London, T. Bewsley, 1808.

History of the Welsh Militia & Volunteer Corps, 1757–1908, Bryn Owen. Bridge Books, Wrexham, 1995.

Lloyd Letters, editor George Eyre Evans, privately printed, 1908.

Princelings, Privilege and Power, Leslie Baker-Jones. Gomer, 1999.

Secret Sins, Sex, Violence & Society in Carmarthenshire, 1870–1920, Russell Davies. University of Wales Press, 1996.

The Changing Face of Medicine in 20th Century Llandysul, Harold Selcon. Llandysul Local History Society, 2003.

The Diary of Thomas Jenkins of Llandeilo, 1826–1870, D. C. Jenkins (editor). Dragon Books, 1976.

The Diary of Sylas Neville, 1767–1788, Basil Cozens-Hardy (editor). Oxford University Press, 1950.

The Other Pepys, Vincent Brome. Weidenfeld & Nicolson, 1992.

The Rake's Diary, Cuwen Archives Trust, 1994.

The South Wales Squires, Herbert M. Vaughan. Methuen & Co., 1926.

They Fought For Themselves, D. Elwyn Davies. Gomer, 1982.

This Small Corner, a History of Pencader and District, Steve Dubé. Carmarthenshire County Council, 2000.

Welsh Folk Customs, Trefor M. Owen. National Museum of Wales/Welsh Folk Museum, Cardiff, 1959.

Welsh Unitarians as Schoolmasters, Rev. David Evans. J. D. Lewis, Gomerian Press, undated.

Y Bywgraffiadur Cymreig Hyd 1940, William Lewis Cyf., Caerdydd.

Newspapers: *Carmarthen Journal*; *The Welshman*.

Internet: Welsh Biography Online, National Library of Wales.

Census: Llanfihangel-ar-Arth; Llandysul; Llanwnnen.

Index

S.T.E.A.M.

THROUGH THE SEASONS

WINTER

ANNA CLAYBOURNE

First published in Great Britain in 2019 by Wayland
Copyright © Hodder and Stoughton 2019

Senior Commissioning Editor: Melanie Palmer
Design: squareandcircus.co.uk
Illustrations: Supriya Sahai

HB ISBN 978 1 5263 0952 5
PB ISBN 978 1 5263 0953 2

Nikolay Antonov/Shutterstock: 9bl. ChameleonsEye/
Shutterstock: 27bc. Dancestrokes/Shutterstock: 17b. FamVeld/
Shutterstock: 5tr. Peter Gudella/Shutterstock: 14br. Jaz_cz/
Shutterstock: 22br. Kikujungboy/Shutterstock: 5cl. Jason
Kolenda/Shutterstock: 20bl. Maya Kruchankova/Shutterstock:
7b. Susan Montgomery/Shutterstock: 25b. Natalya Onishchenko/
Shutterstock: 6bl. prokopphoto/Shutterstock: 27bl. sirtravelalot/
Shutterstock: 29tl. StockPhotoAstur/Shutterstock: 11tr.
Kuttelvaserova Stuchelova/Shutterstock: 27br. Vasillis Ververidis/
Shutterstock: 19b. Additional illustrations: Freepik

Every attempt has been made to clear copyright. Should
there be any inadvertent omission please apply to the
publisher for rectification.

Printed in China

Wayland
An imprint of
Hachette Children's Group
Part of Hodder and Stoughton
Carmelite House
50 Victoria Embankment
London EC4Y 0DZ

An Hachette UK Company
www.hachette.co.uk

SAFETY INFORMATION:
Please ask an adult for help with
any activities that could be tricky,
involve cooking or handling
glass. Ask adult permission when
appropriate.

Due care has been taken to ensure
the activities are safe and the
publishers regret they cannot
accept liability for any loss or
injuries sustained.

Contents

WINTER!

Winter is the coldest, darkest time of the year. The days grow shorter, the nights grow longer and, in some places, the weather can be rainy, snowy and icy. As it gets colder, we have to wrap up in warm clothes, switch on the heating and snuggle up in extra blankets.

Nature in winter

Winter affects plants and animals, too. Some trees lose their leaves, and plants lose their flowers and fruits. You see fewer animals around. Some animals hibernate, spending the winter snoozing in a burrow or den. Many birds fly away to spend the winter somewhere warmer.

WHAT IS WINTER?

Like all the seasons, winter happens because of the way the Earth moves around the Sun.

The Earth orbits around the Sun once every year.

The Earth is tilted. As it moves around, different areas lean more towards the Sun.

When your part of the world is leaning away from the Sun, it's winter where you live!

Autumn
Spring
Winter
Summer
Sun
Summer
Winter
orbit
Spring
Earth
Autumn

Winter festivals

The very shortest day of the year is called the winter solstice. In the Northern Hemisphere it's around the 21 December, and in the Southern Hemisphere, 21 June.

People around the world hold traditional celebrations around this time, including Christmas and New Year in the Northern Hemisphere. There are more modern festivals too, like the Harbin Snow and Ice Sculpture Festival in Harbin, northern China.

Th brights lights of the Harbin Snow Festival in China.

Children decorate a Christmas tree.

Winter science

This book is full of fun science experiments, activities and things to make in winter.

You can do most of them with everyday craft materials and recycled objects from around the house. Turn to page 30 for some extra tips about materials and where to find them.

HAVE AN ADULT HANDY!

SOME OF THE ACTIVITIES INVOLVE SHARP OBJECTS, HEAT AND COOKING. MAKE SURE YOU ALWAYS HAVE AN ADULT TO HELP YOU, AND ASK THEM TO DO THESE PARTS.

MAKE YOUR OWN FROST

In some parts of the world, winter is so cold it brings snow, ice and frost. In others, it's not cold enough for frost ... but you can still make your own!

WHAT YOU NEED:

- AN EMPTY, CLEANED-OUT TIN CAN
- ICE CUBES OR CRUSHED ICE
- SALT
- A SPOON
- GLOVES (OPTIONAL)

Step 1:

Fill the tin can about ¾ full with ice. (Be careful to avoid any sharp edges on the can.)

In a cold winter, frost can form on freezing cold grass, trees, and other objects such as car windscreens.

Winter science: What is frost?

The air always contains some water vapour (water in the form of a gas). When air touches a freezing cold surface, some of this water sticks to the surface and freezes into frost.

When you add salt to ice, it lowers the freezing point of the ice, which makes it start to melt. This takes energy, so the ice takes heat energy from the can, making its temperature fall to below freezing – and so frost forms.

Step 3:

Put the can down and look carefully at the bottom half of it. You should see white, icy frost starting to form on the outside.

If it doesn't work very well indoors, try it outdoors.

Step 2:

Add a large handful of salt, and stir it into the ice. Hold the can near the top, and shake it from side to side for a few seconds.

What else can I do?

As frost forms on objects, it makes crystals in interesting shapes and patterns. If you have a magnifying glass, try taking a close-up look at your frost. You can do the same if you find frost on a window, leaf or grass.

GLOWING IN THE DARK

For thousands of years, people have used candles and lamps, and then electric lighting, to brighten up winter nights. But did you know there are some other, much more unusual ways to make light?

WHAT YOU NEED:

- SUGAR CUBES OR SUGARY HARD SWEETS (MINTS WORK WELL)
- A CLEAR, SEALABLE SANDWICH BAG
- A PAIR OF PLIERS (AND AN ADULT TO HELP)
- STICKING PLASTERS, OR A ROLL OF STRONG STICKY TAPE
- A TOTALLY DARK ROOM

EXPERIMENT 1

Step 1:

Put the sugar cubes or sweets into the bag and seal it closed. Take the bag, an adult and the pliers into the dark room. Wait a few minutes for your eyes to adjust to the dark.

Step 2:

Ask the adult to use the pliers to crush and crunch the sugar or sweets through the bag. Look carefully – can you see them light up?

Step 1:

For another experiment, take the sticking plasters or sticky tape into the room. Hold the end of the tape or the backing paper of a plaster.

Step 2:

While watching closely, quickly rip the tape off the roll, or the backing off the plaster. You might be able to see sparks of light.

What else can I do?

You could try these methods too:

- Stretch an elastic band to and fro - it may start to glow
- Crunch a sugar cube or sweet in your mouth and look in a mirror.
- Seal up a sticky self-seal envelope, then peel it apart again.

Winter science: Sugar sparks

This type of light is called 'triboluminescence'. It happens when some materials are crushed or ripped apart, but scientists are not sure how it works.

BOTTLE BIRD FEEDER

Some birds fly away to warmer places for the winter, but others stay behind. There's not much food around for them, but you can help them out by making a bottle bird feeder.

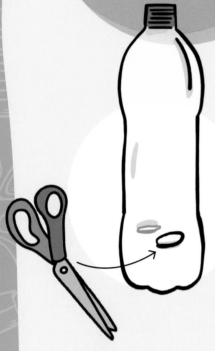

Step 1:

Ask an adult to cut two holes near the bottom of the bottle, opposite each other. The holes should be about 2 cm across.

Step 2:

Push the wooden spoon handle through the holes, so that the spoon part is facing upwards, next to one of the holes.

WHAT YOU NEED:

- A LARGE, CLEAN PLASTIC DRINKS BOTTLE WITH A LID
- AN OLD WOODEN SPOON
- A SHARP CRAFT KNIFE OR SCISSORS (AND AN ADULT TO HELP)
- STRING
- A FUNNEL
- A BAG OF BIRD SEED

Step 3:

Remove the lid. Put the funnel in the top of the bottle, and pour in the bird seed. Fill the bottle up enough to hold the spoon in place. Screw the lid on.

Step 4:

Cut a piece of string about 1 m long and tie one end tightly around the neck of the bottle.

Tie the other end of the string to a low tree branch, washing line or somewhere similar, so that the bird feeder can hang down freely.

Winter science:
Why do some birds stay?

Flying somewhere warmer for the winter takes a lot of energy. So some birds stay, and have other ways of surviving. They may grow extra-warm plumage. Some, including jays (photo above), store a supply of food, like squirrels do.

What else can I make?

For an even easier bird feeder, thread loop-shaped breakfast cereal on to pipe cleaners, bend them into a circle or other shape, and hang up outside.

FROZEN BUBBLES

Bubbles only last a few seconds before they pop. But if it's cold enough, you can actually freeze a bubble. If winter isn't freezing cold where you live, you can use a freezer.

Before you start:

First, mix a teaspoon of glycerin and a teaspoon of sugar into your bubble mixture. This isn't essential, but it helps the bubbles to last longer.

WHAT YOU NEED:

- BUBBLE MIXTURE AND WAND
- GLYCERIN (FROM A PHARMACY OR THE BAKING AISLE IN A SUPERMARKET) (OPTIONAL)
- SUGAR (OPTIONAL)
- A SMALL PLATE
- A DRINKING STRAW
- FREEZING COLD WEATHER, OR A FREEZER

THE OUTDOOR METHOD:

Step 1:

Choose a day that's icy cold, but not windy or rainy. Go outside with your bubble mixture. Carefully blow a bubble and catch it on the wand.

Step 2:

Hold the bubble up and watch closely to see it freeze over.

THE FREEZER METHOD:

Step 1:

First, make a space for your plate in the freezer. Pour a small pool of bubble mixture on to the plate.

Step 2:

Using the straw, blow gently into the bubble mixture to make a bubble on the plate.

Water molecules move freely

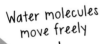

Step 3:

Carefully put the plate in the freezer and close the door. Leave it for a few minutes to freeze.

Winter science:
Why do bubbles pop?

A bubble is made of a thin film of soap and water, with air inside. Air pushes equally in all directions, making the bubble round. But as gravity pulls the water and soap downwards, the film gets thinner, until it pops.

When liquid freezes, its molecules (the units it is made of) move less, and get fixed in place, so the bubble doesn't pop.

Ice molecules are bound together

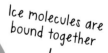

What else can I do?

What happens if you try to break your frozen bubble?

13

ICE BALLOONS

What does the inside of a balloon look like when the balloon isn't there? Make an ice balloon to find out, and use it as an outdoor decoration.

WHAT YOU NEED:

- BALLOONS
- SCISSORS
- WATER
- FOOD COLOURING
- A FUNNEL
- FREEZING COLD WEATHER OR A FREEZER

Step 1:

Stretch the opening of a balloon over the narrow end of the funnel, and run water from the tap into the funnel.

Winter science:
Freezing and melting

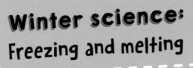

The freezing point of water is 0°C, or 32°F. At this temperature, the molecules in water slow down and become fixed together into a solid. Below freezing temperature, your ice balloon should stay solid. If it starts to melt, you'll know the temperature is above freezing.

Step 2:

When the balloon is full of water, add a few drops of food colouring in your favourite colour. Tie a knot in the neck of the balloon.

Step 3:

Leave the balloon to freeze outdoors, if the temperature is below freezing. If not, put it in a freezer for at least 24 hours.

Step 4:

When the water is frozen solid, use scissors to snip the tied end off the balloon, and peel it off the ice.

What else can I do?

Put an outdoor battery-powered candle or LED click light in a small bowl, or in a hollow scooped in the snow, and sit the ice balloon on top. It will glow with coloured light.

Step 5:

Make as many ice balloons as you like, to decorate a garden or pathway.

BLUBBER GLOVES

If you fell into icy cold water, you'd soon be much too cold. But some animals, like orcas, penguins and polar bears, can easily cope with super-cold conditions. This experiment shows how!

WHAT YOU NEED:

- TWO PLASTIC SANDWICH BAGS
- A PACKET OF BEEF SUET OR VEGETARIAN SUET (FROM A SUPERMARKET)
- A LARGE BOWL
- WATER
- ICE CUBES
- SALT

Step 1:
Open one of the sandwich bags, and pour suet into it until it's almost full. Leave the other bag empty.

Step 2:
Half-fill the bowl with cold water, and add plenty of ice cubes. Then sprinkle in a handful of salt.

Step 3:
Put one of your hands into the suet-filled bag, with your hand in the middle so that it's surrounded by suet. Put your other hand into the empty plastic bag.

Step 4:

Put both hands into the bowl of water (keeping the openings of the bags above water level, so your hands stay dry). How long can you hold your hands in the icy cold water for?

What else can I do?

Try the same experiment using water, flour or sugar instead of suet. Do they work?

Winter science:
Fat blanket

You probably found that the hand surrounded by suet stayed warmer for longer. Suet is made of fat, which works like a blanket to hold heat in. Seals, whales and polar bears have a thick layer of fat, called blubber, under their skin, to help their bodies to stay warm in the cold.

Seals have blubber under their skin.

SLIPPERY SLOPE

In freezing winter weather, the ground can become coated in ice, making it seriously slippery to walk on or drive on. This experiment shows you how to get a grip on the ice.

WHAT YOU NEED:

- A LARGE, SHALLOW TRAY OR BAKING TRAY
- A JUG OF WATER
- A FREEZER OR FREEZING OUTDOOR WEATHER
- PEBBLES
- SMALL PLASTIC TOY FIGURES
- SAND
- SALT

Step 1:

If the temperature is below freezing, put the tray outdoors on a flat surface. If not, put the tray inside a freezer, on a flat shelf.

Carefully pour water into the tray to cover the bottom, and leave it to freeze for at least 3 hours.

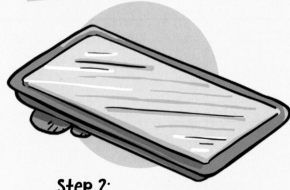

Step 2:

When the water has frozen solid, take the tray out and prop it up on a few pebbles so that it slopes downhill.

Step 3:

Put some toy people on the icy slope and see if you can get them to stand still.

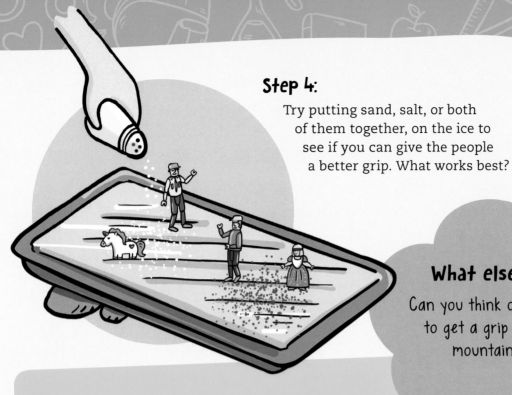

Step 4:

Try putting sand, salt, or both of them together, on the ice to see if you can give the people a better grip. What works best?

What else can I do?

Can you think of any other ways to get a grip on ice? How do mountaineers do it?

Winter science:
Types of sand

Amazingly, scientists still aren't totally sure why ice is so slippery. They think that some of the molecules, or tiny particles, on the surface of ice are slightly "loose", and roll and slide across the surface, making it hard to grip.

When you add sand, it digs into the ice, making it easier to grip. When you add salt, it lowers the freezing point of the ice, making it melt faster.

Gritting lorries spread salt on icy roads to make them less slippery.

FIREWORKS IN A JAR

These 'fireworks' are easy to make, and unlike real fireworks, you can watch them indoors. They are also underwater and upside-down!

WHAT YOU NEED:
- A GLASS JAR OR TUMBLER
- WARM TAP WATER
- COOKING OIL
- LIQUID FOOD COLOURING IN SEVERAL COLOURS

Step 1:
Fill the jar or tumbler ¾ full with warm tap water, and stand it on a flat surface.

Winter science: Oil and water

Water and oil are different types of liquids, and they don't mix together easily. The oil is lighter than the water, so it settles in a layer on top. Food colouring is mostly made of water, too, so it doesn't mix with the oil. Instead, it sinks down through the oil. When it reaches the warm water underneath, it can mix in easily. So it "explodes" and spreads out quickly, making streaks and patterns.

Step 2:
Carefully pour some cooking oil on to the water until there is a layer of oil about 1 cm deep.

Step 3:
Drop a single drop of food colouring on to the oil, and watch what happens.

Step 4:
Add more drops of food colouring, using different colours, to make patterns like a firework display.

What else can I make?
Try filming your fireworks, using the video function on a smartphone or tablet. Then you can watch the video upside down, to see the fireworks exploding upwards!

FAKE SNOW

When film directors want to shoot a snowy scene and there's no snow, they call in a fake snow company. This fake snow is easy to make and looks amazingly realistic.

WHAT YOU NEED:

- A MIXING BOWL
- A PACKET OF CORNSTARCH (CORNFLOUR)
- A CAN OF SHAVING FOAM

Step 1:

Tip the cornstarch into the mixing bowl, carefully so that it doesn't fly around too much.

Winter science: Wet and dry snow

All snow is make of tiny ice crystals, which clump into larger snowflakes. But some snow sticks together easily, and some is very dry and powdery. "Wet" snow falls when the air is above freezing temperature, and the snow is partly melted, making it stickier. Dry snow, or powder, falls when the air is below freezing, and is mostly solid.

By adding more shaving foam, you make the fake snow wetter, until it's damp enough to stick together.

Step 2:

Squirt an apple-sized blob of shaving foam into the cornstarch. Use your hands to mix the ingredients together.

Step 3:

Add more shaving foam, a little at a time, until the mixture looks and feels similar to snow (except not as cold!).

Step 4:

You can roll and clump the fake snow together and make snowballs and snow people.

What else can I make?

- Try putting some fake snow in the freezer for an hour to make it cold. Does it still work?

- Use your snow to make a setting for some toy figures. Pose them for photos, or make a winter film.

GLITTERY SNOW GLOBE

When you shake a snow globe, it fills with a whirling blizzard of snow. It's easy to make your own version with glitter.

WHAT YOU NEED:

- A SMALL GLASS JAR WITH A TIGHT-FITTING SCREW-ON LID
- WHITE MODELLING CLAY
- PLASTIC TOY FIGURES
- STRONG, WATERPROOF GLUE OR A GLUE GUN
- WATER
- A TEASPOON
- GLYCERIN (FROM A PHARMACY OR THE BAKING AISLE OF A SUPERMARKET) (OPTIONAL)
- WHITE GLITTER (OR SILVER IF YOU CAN'T FIND WHITE)

Step 1:

Turn the lid of your jar upside down, and use white modelling clay to make a snowy mound in the middle. Leave the edges clear so the lid can still screw on.

Step 2:

Use strong glue or a glue gun (with an adult to help) to glue the modelling clay to the lid. Arrange your toy figures on the modelling clay, and glue them down too.

Step 3:

Fill the jar with cold water, and stir in 2-3 teaspoons of glitter. If you have it, stir in a teaspoon of glycerin too. This helps the glitter to move around more slowly.

Step 4:

Turn the lid over and carefully fit the lid and winter scene into the jar. Screw the lid on tightly. Shake the jar to start the snowstorm!

What else can I make?

Use colourful glitter for a disco snow globe!

Winter science:
Blizzard warning!

The swirling snowstorm inside a snow globe can happen in real life, and it's called a blizzard. A blizzard is a combination of heavy snowfall and strong wind, filling the air with fast-moving snowflakes. Blizzards can be dangerous, as they make it hard to see where you're going. People sometimes get lost and stuck in the snow.

WINTER CRYSTALS

Salt crystals aren't made of real ice, but they look icy and sparkly. Try growing your own to make frosty-looking winter decorations.

WHAT YOU NEED:

- A PACKET OF EPSOM SALTS (FROM A PHARMACY)
- A CLEAN GLASS JAR
- HOT WATER
- A SPOON
- A MEASURING JUG
- PIPE CLEANERS
- SEWING THREAD
- A PENCIL OR CHOPSTICK

Step 1:

Half-fill the glass jar with Epsom salts, and pour it into the jug. Now half-fill the jar with very hot water from the tap, and pour that in too.

Step 2:

Stir the mixture for at least two minutes, until all or most of the salt has dissolved and disappeared.

Step 3:

Carefully pour the mixture out of the jug into the clean glass jar. If there is any undissolved salt at the bottom of the jug, make sure you leave it behind.

Step 4:

Use a pipe cleaner to make a shape such as a snowflake or star. Tie a short piece of sewing thread to it, and tie the other end to the middle of the pencil or chopstick.

Step 5:

Lower the shape into the jar, resting the pencil or chopstick on top, so that the shape dangles into the mixture.

Winter science:
What are crystals?

Crystals are the natural shapes that some substances take when they can form freely. As the Epsom salts in the water start to clump together again, they grow in a crystal shape.

Step 6:

Put the jar in the fridge, and leave it for at least 24 hours. Crystals should start to form and cover the shape.

Ice crystals

Epsom salts crystals

What else can I make?

Try making crystal-covered leaves, seashells or other shapes.

Table salt crystals

Ice and table salt also form crystals. Each material has its own crystal shape.

CONSTELLATION CARDS

As the nights are long and dark, winter is a good time to look at the stars. On a clear night, you could see several constellations, or star patterns. Or if it's cloudy, recreate them indoors, with these constellation cards.

WHAT YOU NEED:
- PLAIN CARD
- SCISSORS
- A PENCIL
- A RULER
- A COCKTAIL STICK OR LARGE NEEDLE
- TORCH (OR A SMARTPHONE TORCH)
- A DARK ROOM

Step 1:
Cut the card into smaller cards about 10-12 cm across. They can be circles, squares or rectangles.

Step 2:
Look up pictures of constellations in an astronomy book, or on the Internet. Choose a constellation you like, and copy the pattern of stars on to your card.

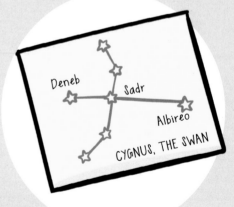

Deneb

Sadr

Albireo

CYGNUS, THE SWAN

Step 3:
Label the card with the name of the constellation. You could add the names of the main stars in it, too.

Winter science:
Why do we only see stars at night?

On a dark, clear night you can see plenty of stars, but in the daytime, they vanish! Actually, though, they are still there. It's just impossible to see them, because light from the Sun (our nearest star) makes the sky too bright.

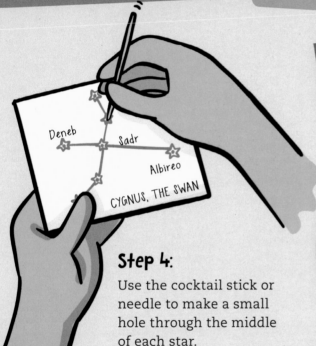

Step 4:
Use the cocktail stick or needle to make a small hole through the middle of each star.

Step 5:
Make cards of all your favourite constellations. To use them, shine a torch at the card in a dark room, so that the constellation appears on the wall.

What else can I make?
Can you use a pattern of pinholes to make a planet, spaceship or comet appear on the wall?

MATERIALS

This list gives you ideas about where to look for the materials you need for the activities in this book.

FROM AROUND THE HOUSE:

- PLIERS
- STICKING PLASTERS
- STRING
- SMALL PLASTIC TOY FIGURES
- COCKTAIL STICKS
- NEEDLE
- TORCH
- COINS

BASIC ART AND CRAFT MATERIALS:

- A SHARP CRAFT KNIFE OR SCISSORS (AND AN ADULT TO HELP)
- SCISSORS
- PENCIL
- RULER
- GLUE
- STICKY TAPE

FROM THE KITCHEN:

- GLASSES, BOWLS, JUGS, SPOONS, PLATES AND SAUCERS
- TRAY
- CHOPSTICKS
- FUNNEL
- FRIDGE
- FREEZER
- SANDWICH BAGS
- PLASTIC BOTTLES
- EMPTY GLASS JARS
- EMPTY TIN CANS
- WATER
- ICE CUBES
- SALT
- SUGAR
- COOKING OIL

FROM A CRAFT OR HOBBY SHOP:

- GLITTER
- STRONG GLUE OR A GLUE GUN
- PIPE CLEANERS
- SEWING THREAD
- PLAIN CARD
- WHITE MODELLING CLAY
- BALLOONS

FROM A GARDEN CENTRE:

- BIRD SEED
- SAND

FROM A SUPERMARKET:

- BUBBLE MIXTURE
- FOOD COLOURING
- SUET
- CORNSTARCH (CORNFLOUR)
- SHAVING FOAM
- STRAWS
- SUGAR CUBES
- HARD SWEETS

FROM A PARK OR GARDEN:

- PEBBLES

FROM A PHARMACY:

- GLYCERIN
- EPSOM SALTS

Glossary

blizzard A snowstorm with lots of snow and strong winds.

blubber A layer of fat under the skin of some sea mammals, such as whales and seals.

constellation A group of stars that appear to form a pattern.

crystals Minerals that have formed in regular, geometric shapes.

freezing point The temperature that a substance freezes at.

frost Ice crystals that form on surfaces in freezing temperatures, from water vapour in the air.

glycerin A thick, colourless, edible liquid, made from natural sources.

hibernate To spend the winter in a sleep-like state.

molecules Tiny units, too small to see, that substances are made up of.

Northern Hemisphere The half of the Earth north of the equator, including the North Pole.

orbit To circle around another object, such as a planet orbiting around the Sun.

plumage A bird's covering of feathers.

Southern Hemisphere The half of the Earth south of the equator, including the South Pole.

triboluminescence Light that is released when some types of substances are crushed, squeezed or stretched.

water vapour Water in the form of a gas. Water vapour is found in the air and released by plants.

winter solstice The day with the shortest number of daylight hours.

Index